To: Daddy
with love from,
Gillian & Brian
x x x

EXETER
IN OLD PHOTOGRAPHS

EXETER

IN OLD PHOTOGRAPHS

COLLECTED BY

PETER THOMAS

ALAN SUTTON
1988

Alan Sutton Publishing Limited
Brunswick Road · Gloucester

First published 1988

British Library Cataloguing in Publication Data

Exeter in old photographs.
1. Devon. Exeter, history
I. Thomas, Peter
942.3′56

ISBN 0-86299-520-5

Typesetting and origination by
Alan Sutton Publishing Limited.
Printed in Great Britain by
WBC Print Limited

CONTENTS

INTRODUCTION	7–9
THE WYKES STUDIO	10–13
VIPs before the studio camera	13–19
POLTIMORE HOUSE	20 & 21
EXETER HOME GUARD	22 & 23
REDHILLS HOSPITAL	24 & 25
GARAGES & VEHICLES IN EXETER	26–37
HOTELS & PUBS	38–60
WILLEYS & BEACH BROS	61–69
SHOPS & STREETS	70–107
INDUSTRIAL & COMMERCIAL BUSINESS	108–115
THE THEATRE ROYAL & THE CIVIC HALL	116–119
ALLHALLOWS CHURCH & ST CATHERINE'S PRIORY	120–121
KENNAWAYS, MOONS & HIGH STREET SHOP WINDOWS	122–129
ST LOYES COLLEGE, THE DEVON AND EXETER INSTITUTION, BODLEY'S FOUNDRY & PAPER MILLS	130–143
SCHOOLS IN THE CITY	144–160

Based on the original work of Henry Wykes and Marjorie Hockmuth.

INTRODUCTION

In 1826 the first permanent photographic image was produced which led to one of the most effective ways of mass communication using a visual image. The incredible impact that photography has had cannot be underestimated. The development of the camera and all the processes surrounding it has played a dramatic role in the history of society over the last 170 years. However, despite modern technology, it is still the human effort and visual concept which ultimately produce great photographs. The pioneer photographers were often trained in the arts, some being traditional artists in their own right, and this training can frequently be seen in the early photographic records.

Despite all modern interpretation of photography, there is still a certain 'wonderment' when an image appears on a blank piece of paper. The camera has certainly been regarded with suspicion, and still is today in some areas of the world – 'the evil eye' as it has been known. The early photographic studio with its enormous wooden cameras, painted backdrops and daylight illumination was revered by many townsfolk. To have your photograph taken was an experience you would not forget and the image was something to be treasured for the rest of your life. The photographer was a highly respected member of the community and it is these men who have been responsible for the preservation of many aspects of our social history. Sometimes a lifetime would be spent recording the facets of a town or city. Often the archive of a local photographer would contain a wide cross-section of material covering portraits, weddings, civic occasions, industry and commercial work and, perhaps, special commissions.

The High Street photographer and large portrait studio have nearly disappeared and in their place has come the freelance photographer who works from home, his material processed by a laboratory and all his needs carried in one small bag. This significant change has come about basically because of the invention of the ubiquitous 35mm camera; whereas one photographer would have undertaken the work in a town, it is now fought for by numerous individuals. It is unfortunate that because of this situation many valuable archives are not being created and maintained.

Exeter in old Photographs is the result of two people's work, with the majority of the material having been taken by Henry Wykes, Exeter's most eminent and long-standing photographer. His last studio was in Northernhay Place and was well-utilised by the local community. This is proved by his well-kept accounts books which detail the dates of nearly all the 42,000 negatives produced by him and Marjorie Hockmuth with whom he worked.

A request from the Director of the Royal Albert Memorial Museum, to exhibit my collection of historical photographic equipment, led to a lifetime interest in the historical photographic records of the city. Henry Wykes had died in 1964 and Marjorie Hockmuth had decided to continue running the studio in Northernhay Place for as long as she could. Marjorie was a charming lady and was always willing to answer any questions that I put to her about photographic processes and general studio work. The huge mahogany and brass camera had pride of place in the studio and at the time the studio closed it was a little unusual to see such pieces still being used. Henry Wykes had died at the age of 90 and Marjorie was then also in her latter years. She still used a wooden half-plate camera and was particularly fond of a Ross wide-angle lens.

My early years in the photographic retail trade wakened an interest in the history of photography and I amassed quite a lot of equipment. The proposed exhibition in the Royal Albert Memorial Museum inspired me to look for photographs taken with equipment that I was about to exhibit. I contacted Marjorie Hockmuth.

'Marjorie, do you have any old photos of Exeter that may be of interest to integrate with some of my old equipment?'

'Oh yes. Come over. I am sure I can help you.'

Upon arrival at the studio, she led me to a small room and opened the door.

'I think you may find something in here,' she said. 'Have a look through and borrow what you want. It's all very old stuff.'

The room contained hundreds of half-plate boxes each filled with celluloid negatives and glass plates. I started opening the boxes; the more I opened, the more extraordinary I found them.

'This can't be Exeter, Marjorie!' I exclaimed.

'Oh yes, they are all Exeter. That is High Street before the war.'

I had lived in Exeter all my life, but here was a city I did not recognise. This was the start of a lifetime interest in preserving historial photographic records of the City of Exeter. Over the years I have increased the collection considerably.

In 1974 the Henry Wykes Studio finally closed and initially I purchased only part of the negative stock. However, after about two years, I finally had an opportunity to put the whole stock back together. Together with the accounts books, it forms a unique record of the City of Exeter.

Henry Wykes was a self-taught photographer, with style and obvious abilities. He was also a specialist in the painting of miniatures and, as a member of the Royal Academy, he exhibited his works on a number of occasions. He had come to

England from Australia and in 1914 took over the well-known Exe Bridge Studio which overlooked the River Exe. From this daylight studio he went to Bedford Circus and, when blitzed, finally went to Northernhay Place, having a basement studio under the offices of a solicitors' business. During the move from Exe Bridge to Bedford Street, many valuable glass plates were lost. Several of these were 20 × 16 in size and some of the earliest photographic records of the city. These were the original negative stock of the Exe Bridge Studio and they were never found.

Here then is a small but varied selection of work, of which the majority is that of Henry Wykes and Marjorie Hockmuth. However, particularly in the section dealing with public houses, records kindly given to me by the well-known archaeologist Arthur Everett supplement the group, completing a fascinating account of some of the city's lost buildings.

THE DATES OF PHOTOGRAPHS

The dates shown on photographs are those shown in the accounts books of the Wykes Studio. It may not be in some cases the actual date on which the record was made. However, it is most unusual to have such an accurate aid to dating photographs. It must be assumed that from at least 1964 all records were taken by Marjorie Hockmuth; Henry Wykes had not in fact taken an active role in the studio for some time before he died.

HENRY WYKES – Photographer 1874 to 1964.
Henry Wykes came to Exeter in 1914 from Australia after practising as an artist and bought the Exe Bridge premises which had been a recognised daylight studio for many years. He had no formal training in photography and while in Exeter he still painted, did copy and restoration work, and hand colouring. Essentially, however, he worked with the camera on many aspects of city life.

THE STUDIO at 4 Northernhay Place attracted many notable clients and VIPs, some of which are presented in this book. The studio, which was a classic example of its type, was in the basement of the building and the room was pannelled. It had a formalised look, but the atmosphere of a comfortable lounge. At all times it was uncluttered. A very small room in one corner was used for the processing of film and plates. Henry Wykes used a photographic printer called 'Mr Burgess'. The Wykes/Hockmuth Studio was the last studio of its type in Exeter and it is unusual and fortunate that these records exist to show how it was laid out. A painted background was utilised and the window shown is false. For portraiture a large lighting trough was used containing sodium lights operating via a transformer. A number of normal household light bulbs supplemented the unit, otherwise any skin imperfections would have been exaggerated, in particular freckles. The effect of this lighting also improved the look of blue eyes, giving them greater impact in the finished print.

TO IMPRESS CLIENTS with the quality of work produced, exhibition prints would be hung in the studio. These would cover many aspects of the studio's work, but portraits predominated. The exhibition prints have been retained and form an integral part of the Isca Collection. In latter years Henry Wykes took a lesser role in the day-to-day work, the majority being undertaken by Miss Hockmuth.

HENRY WYKES WAS A SKILLED PAINTER OF MINIATURES and was a member of the Royal Institute of Miniature Painters. He was recognised for his work and on a number of occasions had his work exhibited in the Royal Academy. Early in his career the artist had spent time in Holland and had an interest in copying old masters whilst staying in Antwerp.

MRS PINDER, 13 June 1966. Chairman, Tavistock Urban District Council.

MR STEELE PERKINS, Sheriff of Exeter from 1956 to 1957, in a portrait taken on 13 February 1959. He was also elected mayor in 1961. The Steele Perkins family achieved a remarkable record relating to public service and the Crown. Councillor Steele's great-great-grandfather, occupied the office of sheriff in 1858; his grandfather in 1880, becoming mayor in 1894; and his father was sheriff in 1913 and mayor in 1928.

ALDERMAN WALTER DAW, Mayor of Exeter from 1963 to 1964. Alderman Daw is one of the most respected and well-known of Exonians. He has always taken a very active role in Exeter life, particularly in education. Born in Paul Street, he was educated at Heles School and has been Chairman of its Board of Governors. His work has included being on the managing bodies of Maynard and Episcopal School, serving on the University Council, being chairman of the Exeter Education Committee and chairman of the Housing Committee, amongst many other activities. The Exeter Amateur Operatic Society has received great support from Alderman Daw, who has always had a passion for stage productions, and has also been chairman of the Western Orchestral Association.

COUNCILLOR G.J. GREENSLADE, Mayor of Exeter from 1955 to 1956. Gilbert John Greenslade was made an alderman in 1952 and was director and manager of the well-known Exeter company Greenslades Tours Ltd.

MR BROWNE, Master of the Guild of Fullers, Tuckers and Shearmen. This Guild is the oldest in Exeter and has its headquarters at Tuckers Hall in Fore Street, one of the city's most historic and beautiful buildings. The Guild is traced back to the very early years of the woollen cloth trade and consisted then of Masters of the trade. Today the Guild is supported by a corps of businessmen who retain the hall and maintain it, but in general the Guild members are no longer associated with any aspect of the cloth trade.

BISHOP DR ROBERT MORTIMORE photographed in the Palace Grounds in Exeter. The Bishop was an avid football supporter and was often seen at the local football ground. Much admired in the city, he was Bishop of Exeter from 1949 to 1973.

THE HIGH SHERIFF OF DEVON Sir Peter W. Hoare of Luscombe Castle, Dawlish.

THE LATE LORD AND LADY CLIFFORD wearing their state robes for the coronation of Queen Elizabeth II. The photograph was taken 24 August 1953 at Lawell House, one mile from Ugbrooke Park, the ancestral family home.

EXTERIOR VIEW OF POLTIMORE HOUSE, 31 May 1960. This fine building was the birthplace for a number of Exeter residents. At one time a private residence, it was converted into a hospital and a nursing home in 1945 by its then owner, Dr Fortescue Folkes. The Bampfylde family had owned the land and house until 1921, the site having been in their possession since the early fourteenth century. The family sold off their assets and the mansion and grounds were the last to go. Two owners maintained the property between 1921 and 1945 and it had an excellent stock of deer in the park up until the Second World War. Between 1945 and 1963 over 10,000 patients were catered for, some 4,674 were national health patients, and in 1963 Poltimore House became an annexe of the Royal Devon and Exeter Hospital.

Top right
POLTIMORE HOUSE – the salon, shown on 31 May 1960, was one of the most beautiful rooms in the house; with white walls and decorated with gold it is in the late seventeenth-century rococo style. The two oval mirrors have carved lime-wood frames with egg and tongue beading and they are surrounded by ribbons and flowers. In the centre of the ceiling is depicted the head of Queen Anne set among floating clouds, the sun's rays radiating from her. It is said that this room dates back to the building's Tudor period and the superb, decorated plasterwork in some of the rooms has been attributed to the Abbots of Frithelstock. John Abbot executed the ceiling in the Custom House at Exeter 1680/1.

BEDROOM IN POLTIMORE HOUSE, 31 May 1960. Known as the 'Gold Room', this bedroom for patients obtained its name from the carved cornices and moulded dado decorated with gold and cream.

EXETER HOME GUARD, A Company, 5 October 1941, with Lieutenant King. During May 1940 Sir Anthony Eden broadcast a message to the people of Britain that volunteers were required to step forward 'to defend the old country from anything which the enemy might attempt to do.' Within a short period of time, over a thousand men had signed on at the police station to do their duty. The local defence volunteers, whose offical title was to be 1st (Loyal City of Exeter) Battalion, Devon Home Guard, was to be split into three companies: No. 1 west, from Cowley Bridge to Pinhoe Road; No. 2 east, from Pinhoe Road to River Exe; and No. 3 St Thomas from the river to Cowley Bridge. At the end of the day up to two thousand men were incorporated into the companies.

EXETER HOME GUARD, 14 September 1941, under the command of Lieutenant Spiller. The early duties of the Home Guard related to patrols and observation posts at Hill Barton Road, Digby Halt, Swing Bridge, Countess Weir, Northbrook Park, Exeter School and the canal banks. Guards were placed at Trews Weir suspension bridge, the electric light works and oil stores. Further guards operated at Admiralty buildings, the city centre, St David's station, Pynes Waterworks, Staffords Bridge and North Bridge. The detachment commander had a small headquarters in Pancras Lane where company commanders' meetings were held. Parades took place in Pancras Lane on Monday, Tuesday and Wednesday evenings.

EXETER HOME GUARD, 18 October 1941. A small school house was utilised in Paul Street as an HQ and training was carried out in the parking ground here and in the Higher Market. Some of the volunteers were old soldiers and some had never held a gun in their lives. Only 60 rifles were available at the start, but a variety of weapons were to be used, including old shotguns, sticks, ancient revolvers and anything that one could defend oneself with. Volunteers undertook to do one night in six besides their training. Sometimes there was little more than a cowshed to sleep in. However these were the early days and things did improve. The service continued for approximately four and a half years.

KEN LARK, No. 2 Section, No. 1 Platoon, No. 2 Company (St James) 1 Battalion, (Loyal City of Exeter) Devon Home Guard. 21 March 1942.

THE REAR OF REDHILLS HOSPITAL showing the fire escape, 11 June 1954. In 1985 this hospital was accused of inadequate fire precautions and in this photograph of 1954 a member of the staff is standing at the top of the rear escape. The building had been known as the St Thomas Poor Law Institution until the 1930s and had been administered by the St Thomas Guardians Committee. It was transferred to the Public Assistance Committee and finally to the South Western Regional Hospital Board on 5 July 1948. In 1951 the chairman of East Devon hospitals group claimed that Redhills Hospital had been developed from a workhouse into a useful and well-run hospital. The hospital was mainly for sick old people and the chronically ill, but it also had a well-equipped maternity section. There were 79 births in 1949 and 175 in 1950.

A newspaper report of 1985 records that the Exeter Health Authority agreed that Redhills Hospital was unsatisfactory and had to be replaced; that plans would be produced for a replacement in the New Year.

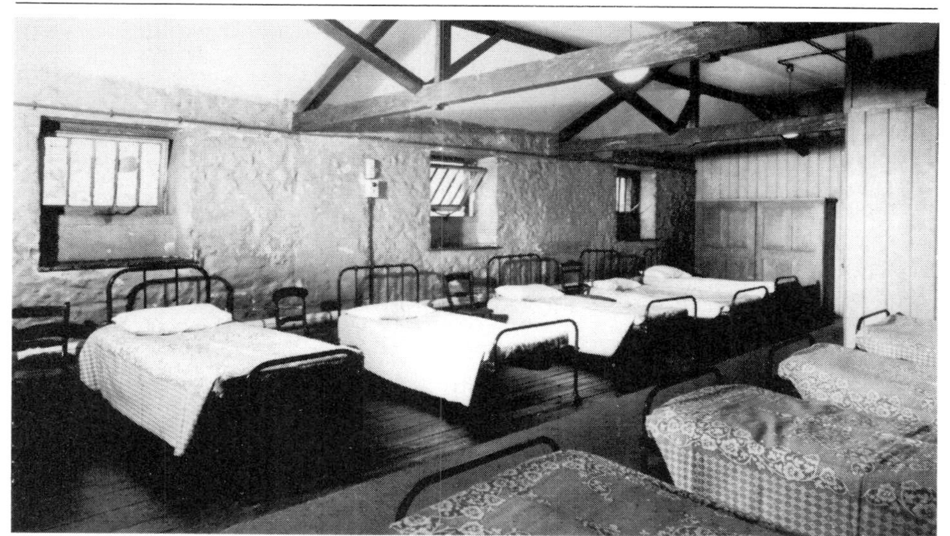

INTERIOR OF REDHILLS HOSPITAL, 11 Janauary 1954. A sad reflection upon the conditions provided for the old and sick.

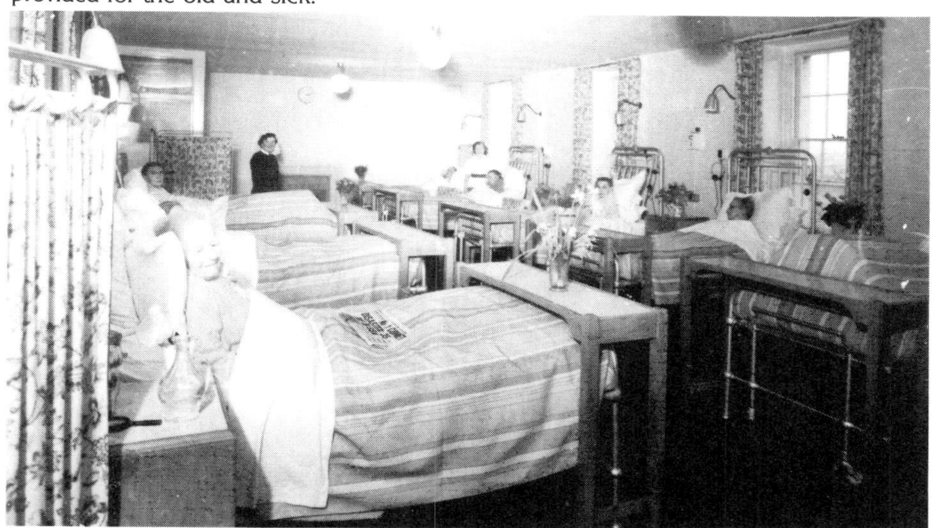

ELDERLY PATIENTS in a ward at Redhills Hospital, 11 January 1954. In June 1970 a new day unit was set up at Redhills Hospital, designed to 'keep elderly people active and useful members of the community.' A budget of £1,500 was allocated for the task. The intention was to keep old people out of hospital, but still with the opportunity to use the day unit for physiotheraphy and occupational therapy. It was considered a far-sighted idea because if old people were left alone their condition would deteriorate and hospital beds would have to be found. Vacant hospital accommodation was used for the purpose. The unit could cater for up to a hundred people per week. It was designed to give old people independence in the community for as long as they lived.

A NEW VAN FOR THE CITY STEAM LAUNDRY supplied by Standfield and White. The City Steam Laundry was situated in Edgerton Park, Pennsylvania Road. The company's advertisements declared 'The van will call on receipt of a postcard'! The City Steam Laundry was used extensively by the Royal Clarence Hotel and undertook the cleaning of all their bed linen. The proprietor welcomed 'vists of inspection from the public'. Mr Martin L. Barnecutt, proprietor, was presented with an award of merit at a National Laundry Association Exhibition and received the gold medal.

CHEAM & DISTRICT AMBULANCE outside the west front of Exeter Cathedral, date unknown.

THE CASTLE, Daimler car and trumpeters, date unknown. Taken in the grounds outside the courts at Exeter Castle, the two trumpeters from the Kings Hussars have been used to announce the arrival of the judge at the High Court sessions. In the past the chauffeur-driven car was a government vehicle, but today's cars are supplied under contract. Trumpeters could be used from various sources including the Marines and Boys' Brigade.

COOMBE STREET, 24 July 1954, showing Gaytons Garage, with Folletts Building in the background and part of Central School to the left. Both structures were demolished. These buildings played important roles in the area of the West Quarter. Central School educated many children from the western side of the city and the large tenement block housed working-class families. The photograph was taken from James Street which came out into Coombe Street. The city wall ran at the back of James Street and many local children would climb onto the wall and look down into houses and gardens in Quay Lane.

REID & LEE GARAGE, New North Road, 5 May 1949. New North Road and Longbrook Street have, until recent times, been the favoured trading place for Reid & Lee, garage and car dealers. Operating since 1905, the initial business was in hire vehicles. This operation was to change to the sales and servicing of new cars. The original partnership of Reid & Evans then changed to Reid & Lee and has remained unaltered to date. Today the building is shown is the Freefit Auto Centre, Reid & Lee operating from Marsh Barton.

THE EARLY DAYS OF CRYPTON TUNING at Reid & Lee, New North Road, 2 May 1950.

THE CITY GARAGE, New North Road, 26 October 1948. At this time the building was occupied by Maudes who earlier in the century had also had a motor mart business in Paris Street specialising in Clyno cars. The old fire station is seen to the immediate left, with Pickfords Removals at the end of the street. On the left of the photograph a hanging sign shows 'Gould and Allen, Family Grocers, Tea and Coffee Dealers'. At this time the garage supplied petrol via two simple pumps on the immediate forecourt.

THE SAME BUILDING AS ABOVE, but trading under the name 'Blue Star Garage', 29 April 1959. The forecourt pumps have been replaced by more up-to-date models. The two attendants are filling up a Renault with petrol and checking the oil. The company advertises a 'Marfax Service Week'. This substantial property now stands in a very poor state and is due for demolition, being replaced by housing for the elderly.

THE SPHINX BUILDING, 5 May 1949. Ever keen to expand, Reid & Lee acquired over the years a number of properties in New North Road from which to conduct their business. The Co-op Garage and some stables were purchased in 1936 leading to the construction of the city's finest car showroom, given the title of the 'Sphinx Building', for in the centre of its pediment is a full-busted sphinx. By today's standards the building would be classifed as very small for the purpose and the present owner operates a secondhand furniture business from it under the name of 'Dickens'. Reid & Lee also occupied No. 34 New North Road which had been the electricity generating station and old fire station.

WHAT IS THE EVENT? 23 July 1941. The showroom is that of Standfield & White in Sidwell Street. The vehicle has a collecting box in front of it with a notice on the screen. Arrangements have been made for visitors to be refreshed with tea and biscuits. Cyclamens and primulas are placed on the table. Two men are inspecting the car while a young man and lady sit having tea, complete with silver cake-stand and teapot.

THE BEDFORD GARAGE, shown here on 30 December 1938, was situated in the middle of Exeter with its main entrance opposite Dellars Cafe in Bedford Street. It was extremely large and totally covered. It offered 'The largest and most convenient parking in the City'. The garage was destroyed in 1942.

KINGS ASPHALT ROAD SURFACING VEHICLE. Kings Asphalt Ltd, based at the Basin Junction Works, were suppliers of building stone, concrete and roadstone, as well as specialising in road surfacing. The company started business in 1928, the works at Basin Junction being constructed in 1929 to manufacture bitumen materials under license from the Anglo American Asphalt Company. The business prospered until the Second World War when demand dropped. In 1933 the company purchased a stone quarry at Burlescombe and supplied material through the Ministry of Transport to American airforce bases during the war. Local authorities became regular customers of Kings Asphalt. In 1983 the company was taken over by Messrs Colas Roads Ltd.

KING & KEARY, shippers and packers, line up their new fleet of removal lorries beside Buller's Statue in New North Road on 23 April 1957. The General seems to be looking on with some displeasure! In the late 1920s King & Keary of 40–1 Sidwell Street ran a bargain shop for furniture and had vans running to and from London each week. The pantechnicons especially constructed for the safe conveyance of furniture were at the customers' service, rates were low and a visit to the showrooms would be greatly esteemed.

THE GAS COMPANY TABLEAU, 16 October 1948. Gas appliances are seen here aboard a small van used for advertising purposes. The pre-war Exeter Gaslight and Coke Company were situated at Nos. 11 and 12 East Southernhay. Their 'motto': 'Gas for everything – to warm a house comfortably, light it pleasantly, ensure cooking that is dependable and hot water in plenty – all without extravagance – is no small achievement. Yet all this can be done using gas. In all, the all-gas house, one servant can do the work of two!'

The van is photographed in Southernhay. The right-hand area shows the north side of Southernhay which was blitzed. On the left is seen the hedge beyond which were the gardens, later removed.

A VAN SUPPLIED BY STANDFIELD & WHITE for the Home and Colonial stores, 23 July 1941. It is thought that this photograph was taken on Prince Charles Road. The right-hand front main light has been covered for wartime black-out purposes. Vans of this nature are once again becoming fashionable.

THE ENTRANCE TO STANDFIELD & WHITE GARAGE, Sidwell Street, 10 September 1952. As one of the major motor engineers in the city, Standfield & White undertook work on Humber, Hillman, Sunbeam Talbot, Commer and Karrier cars as a main agent for the Rootes Group. The corner of the London Inn Square had been blitzed in 1942 leaving the property of Standfield & White as the first premises on the left-hand side of Sidwell Street. At the rear can be seen the structure of the theatre as it stretches down Longbrook Street.

BREWERY WAGONS would have been a fairly common sight in the West Quarter. The date of this photograph copied by Wykes is unknown.

A BREWERY WAGON in Exe Island. The shape of the bridge through which Exe Island was entered from Frog Street can be seen in the background. The bridge was demolished to allow Western Way to continue to the River Exe.

THE TRIANGLE CAR PARK, 28 January 1964. The area shown, known as 'The Triangle', takes its name from the shape of the area of land, defined by a fence and trees, from which the photograph was taken. To the left of the photograph is the Axminster Inn which marked the end of the old Paris Street. Where, at the rear, W.H. Smith Wholesalers are shown, pre-war gardens, houses and small businesses had previously existed: Russell Street was on the right and Paris Street to the left. Almost all these buildings were lost in the Second World War. On the end of the Axminster Inn were a hairdresser and newsagents, 'A B Rouse', and immediately behind it the only building left of the old Russell Street.

THE ROYAL CLARENCE HOTEL in St Peter's Churchyard, at one time simply known as 'The Hotel', can boast to be the first hotel in England. It has also gone under the name of The Clarence and Thompsons Hotel. In 1815 a meeting was held here to discuss how to light Exeter by gas and Exeter was the first place in the county to adopt the new invention. There are few hotels in England that can offer such magnificent views of an English cathedral from its windows.

THE ROYAL CLARENCE COCKTAIL BAR, 26 September 1950. 'Shaken or stirred sir?' The Royal Clarence provided the city with its first cocktail bar, called the Zodiac Bar, opened in 1939. Fifty-one different cocktails were available with exotic names such as Ladies' White, Blue and Brown, Kentucky Colonel, Commodore, Doctor, Old Etonian, Tugboat Annie and, an extra speciality, The Corpse Reviver. Great emphasis was placed on the customers' comfort and the decor was pink Vitrolite with a fireplace in satin silver surrounded by signs of the zodiac. Mr Ginger Wood, manager of the bar, and an expert in dispensing cocktails, won acclaim for his Gloom Chaser.

THE ROYAL CLARENCE HOTEL. The room shown here on 6 February 1958 has been referred to in the past as 'The Drake Lounge' and was at one time part of the Exeter Bank and also Dellers Cafe. It was recently completely refurbished and named Orchards. Today (1988) the whole hotel is having an extensive refurbishment, the like of which it has never seen. To meet the demands and needs of today's clientele, several million pounds are being spent to up-grade the building.

BAR AT THE ROYAL CLARENCE HOTEL, 6 February 1958. After the turn of the century, the Royal Clarence possessed numerous antiques which wer placed throughout the building and the hotel produced an excellent booklet in which were listed all the items to be found within. Some 468 items, many of them having some relevance to Exeter, included plates, swords, letters, statues, documents, helmets, breastplates, spears, shields, tankards, candlesticks, clocks, mace racks, guns, engravings and paintings.

THE ROYAL CLARENCE HOTEL. As seen from its inventory of antiques and items of interest there were some items which were worthy of special attention. Item 300 'Quaint figures' is said to represent Sir Jeffery Hudson and his wife. Born in Oakham, Rutland in 1619, Hudson was a dwarf who won royal favour after being taken into the service of the Duchess of Buckingham when 9 years old. At a visit of Charles I and Henrietta Maria, the Duchess startled the couple by releasing Hudson from a pie at a dinner given in their honour. So bemused was the queen that she offered him the opportunity to join her in service where he became a firm court favourite. He died in 1692, after growing to a mere 3ft. 6in.

EXTERIOR VIEW OF THE ROYAL CLARENCE HOTEL, 28 May 1953. The hotel is flying the Union Jack and flags are also hanging in Martins Lane to celebrate the coronation. At this time parking was allowed in the Cathedral Close, but today traffic has been almost completely eliminated owing to the redesigning of the area. The large canopy over the front entrance of the hotel hides its original portico, the canopy being a very much later edition.

THE ELEPHANT HOTEL, North Street, *c.*1960. The hotel stood halfway down Fore Street on the right-hand side and was adjacent to No. 38 North Street – Messrs Mansfields antique dealers, reproductions, house-furnishers, cabinet-makers and upholsterers. Both buildings were demolished as part of the Guildhall shopping precinct development. In particular the loss of No. 38 was tragic as it was one of the city's most historic and interesting buildings.

THE IMPERIAL HOTEL is fortunate in possessing some of the most extensive and finest grounds in the City of Exeter. Early advertisements describe the Imperial Hotel as 'The Only Hotel in Exeter standing in its own beautiful grounds of over 6 acres'. This handsome Georgian building still retains the air of a private country house, but combines with the advantages of the city. The dates of photographs are unknown.

THE IMPERIAL HOTEL, once known as 'Elmfield House', faces south and overlooks well-established gardens. Henry Wykes was commissioned to capture some of the character of the grounds – the pond and fountains are shown here.

A DELIGHTFUL SEAT in the garden, shaded by magnificent cedars and firs, was greatly appreciated by visitors to the hotel.

THE IMPERIAL HOTEL'S AMPLE GARDENS provided at one time the majority of fresh vegetables for the table together with the salad. Delicious dessert fruits were available throughout the season from the Peach House and vineries. The building was advertised as being 'electrically lighted' in 1928.

THE CONSERVATORY is perhaps the most famous feature of the Imperial Hotel. Originally sited at Streatham Hall, the structure was removed and re-erected on this site. It is attributed to Isambard Kingdom Brunel and is said to be one of his standard designs.

A RELAXED AND CALM ATMOSPHERE was the trademark of the Imperial Hotel with thanks due to the 'Imperial Orchestra' which played in the lounge during the summer months. 'The individual comforts of all guests are studied and prompt attention is given to every detail', it was claimed.

DINING ROOM, the Imperial Hotel.

LOOKING FROM THE SUMMER HOUSE to the hotel. At one time the view from the hotel would have shown Exwick as no more than a handful of buildings, behind which extended the unhindered green fields of Devon. It is not the case today as most of the land in and around Exwick has lost its rural character.

THE PORT ROYAL, 1 January 1954. This waterside public house is shown here before its modern refurbishment. It is probable that the pub, dating from mid-Victorian times, is in fact made up of a number of waterside cottages and it is one of the few places in Exeter that has been involved with a whirlwind! A raging wind picked up a vessel into the air, dashing it down again into the water, much to the amazement of the onlookers. To the right behind the pub is seen Exe House, a villa and the high spire of St Leonard's church.

THE VICTORY INN, Sidwell Street, 1 January 1954. On the right-hand side of Sidwell Street as he left the London Inn, Inn Square, in 1954, the visitor would have seen the above properties. The company of W. French and Co. was established in 1833 and came into Exeter from Pynes Mill prior to the construction of the new City Waterworks. Specialising in animal feedstuffs, seeds and fertilisers, the company, which is still trading today, is very well-known in the city and county. The two shops on the corner of Sidwell Street were destroyed in 1942, but business continued in temporary premises for 20 years. A new store, from which the company trades today, was built in 1962. The Victory Inn, together with adjoining shops, was demolished as part of the redevelopment on Sidwell Street in the early 1960s.

THE VALIANT SOLDIER INN was demolished in 1962 as part of the new road-widening scheme for the continuation of Western Way down to the River Exe. The inn was recorded back to 1670. Before the inn's construction, the site had lain empty for about 30 years. An inn called 'The Golden Lion' had been demolished to give a clear view of the city walls pending the siege of Fairfax. The name 'Valiant Soldier' is said to derive from the Civil Wars. The building had a large yard for the hitching of horse and carts. With the decline of the woollen industry, the road traffic diminished and the Valiant Soldier's yard became under-used. This junction with Holloway Street, Magdalen Road and South Street formed a wonderful setting of historic buildings that were totally swept away. Outside the inn was an underground toilet, a horse trough (still in the Council Yard) which is inscribed, and a telephone box. Next to the Valiant Soldier Inn was Warnes Cycles.

THE GREYHOUND, Sidwell Street, 22 April 1958. With the post-war rebuilding of Exeter came another style of public house. Today known as the Printers' Pie, taking its name from the fact that it is next to the local newspaper offices, this pub was initially known as 'The Greyhound'. Although a large establishment, the building's interior lacked character and was of a utilitarian nature. In recent years the public house has changed its internal character and today displays artificial beams, giving a completely different decor from the original design. It is unfortunate that this period of architecture in the city left little that was desirable.

THE HALF MOON INN, Alphington Street, c.1960. It was demolished to make way for road improvements.

THE ROYAL OAK, Alphington Street, 1 January 1954. It was demolished in advance of part of the Exe Bridge road-improvement scheme.

THE CROWN AND SCEPTRE standing at the Exeter end of the Iron Bridge provided an excellent stopping-off place for many of the wagons and carts which came into the city from the country to sell their wares. Having a large yard at the rear, large numbers could be accommodated. As the woollen trade went into a decline road traffic became less, but the Crown and Sceptre in latter times even attracted village buses and farmers' vehicles. The original building was probably built on this site in the seventeenth or early eighteenth century. The property shown dates from 1835, the Iron Bridge being constructed in 1834. This classic commercial hotel of the period still retains its Victorian portico.

THE PACK HORSE INN takes its name from the heyday of Exeter's woollen trade. Making their way to the North Gate, pack horse drivers would probably have stopped their teams here before proceeding into the city. A great deal of traffic had always used this route when bringing their goods in from the country before the construction of Queen Street and the Higher Market. In 1963 a china jug was found by workmen under the floorboards of a house in Bystock Terrace. It bore the inscription 'Elizabeth Elmore, Pack Horse Inn, Exeter'. The jug was given to the landlord, Mr W.G. Kirkby. Not knowing its origin, he contacted the local *Express & Echo*, and an article provoked a response from Charles Warren, former city alderman and mayor from 1930–1931. He was 90 at the time. Elizabeth Elmore was his great-grandmother and his great-grandfather had run the Pack Horse Inn. The jug was presented to Mr Warren as a family keepsake.

THE LORD NELSON INN, Topsham, 1 January 1954. The public house shown has been subject to a lot of changes since this photograph was taken. In very recent times the emphasis has been on promoting an attractive visual display for its customers and in 1988 it won the City Award for the best-kept garden for hotels, pubs or restaurants.

THE POLTIMORE ARMS, 1 January 1954.

THE CLIFTON INN, Newtown, Christmas decorations, 5 January 1955. During its lifetime the Clifton Inn has been substantially expanded and today has incorporated into it a house and two cottages. The entrance to the cellar is found in the middle of the lounge floor. It is interesting to note that the present landlord's cat and dog will go nowhere near it, even if carried. It has been suggested by the locals that the cellar was, or is, haunted. However, to date, no apparitions have appeared to put the customers off their alchoholic refreshment!

ST ANNE'S WINES AND SPIRITS, 1 January 1954. An unnamed off-licence in Exeter with an Odeon poster on its side wall. Do you know where it is?

COUNTESS WEAR HOTEL, 15 April 1954. Today known as the Exeter Moat House Hotel, the Countess Wear Hotel was originally situated very near Countess Wear Bridge, on the site of Martins Caravans. The hotel shown was the replacement built in the mid-1930s. Extensive road improvements took place at this time which included the widening of Countess Wear Bridge in 1936.

IN THE AREA KNOWN AS EXE ISLAND, two inns existed in close proximity to each other. The Shakespeare Inn stood on the edge of Bonhay Road with the Cattle Market Inn almost directly behind it. The lower leat which flowed along the edge of Bonhay Road separated them. As its name implies the Cattle Market Inn was frequented by cattlemen who came into the Cattle Market which stood on the other side of Bonhay Road, on the very edge of the river. Cattle dealers visiting the abbattoir would also pen their cattle and go for a drink at the inn to discuss business. Traced back to the beginning of the nineteenth century, the Cattle Market Inn was named as a place for undesirables. A report following a murder trial informed the public that 'The deceased had spent the night in disreputable company, both male and female, in the Cattle Market Inn, and had been followed home through the streets.'

THE PLYMOUTH INN, Alphington Street, *c.*1960. A further Exeter Inn was to disappear with the rebuilding of St Thomas as part of the Exe Bridge development scheme.

THE ACORN INN originally stood a short distance from the entrance to Southernhay on the south side of Magdalen Road. The inn actually faced the city mortuary at the rear of the old Royal Devon and Exeter Hospital. It was perhaps a sobering thought for clients not to over-indulge! A very small building, the Acorn Inn would have been typical of the kind of drinking houses that existed in the city at one time. Many drinking places would have been no larger than average sitting-rooms. This tiny public house, which had tiling half-way up its frontage, was incorporated between a number of early buildings, courtyards and alleyways. This area of Exeter had at the time an atmosphere all of its own. Unfortunately today there is no indication of what was once a unique area of the city. *c.* 1960.

THE SHAKESPEARE INN stood in Bonhay Road opposite the old Cattle Market. With the construction of the Exe Bridges and the creation of the Western Way traffic system, the inn, standing in the way of progress, was demolished. Behind the Shakespeare Inn ran the lower leat on whose edge stood the Cattle Market Inn. Perhaps the leat was used to cool off clients from both premises if things got out of hand! c.1960.

THE BULLERS ARMS, Alphington Road, c.1960. Amongst a number of properties that were demolished in St Thomas was the Bullers Arms, which was mentioned in an article in 1970 describing 'the biggest demolition scheme ever carried out since the blitz.' The loss of this section of the city was due to the second phase of the new twin Exe Bridge scheme. This was the first pub of three that was demolished. Its name was taken from Exeter's famous General.

SAWYERS ARMS, Preston Street, c.1960. The Sawyers Arms stood at he top of Preston Street at the junction with Market Street and opposite Gendon Buildings. At the top of the road was Sun Street which led to South Street. The road was to be obliterated with the post-war rebuilding scheme. The site of the Sawyers Arms is today the grass area on the right as you enter from Market Street. Until very recently it was the site of the RSPCA premises.

THE WONFORD INN, *c.*1960.

THE BRIDGE INN, Ide, on 1 January 1954. Now the Twisted Oak. For many Exonians the village of Ide provided the nearest contact with country life. Leaving the centre of Exeter, crossing the river and continuing along Cowick Street and up Dunsford Hill, the walker turned left at the top and proceeded down Little John Cross Hill, where a small pub called the Bridge Inn greeted him. Still serving customers today, the small country public house has been dislocated from the village of Ide by a newly-constructed road scheme.

THE BISHOP BLAIZE INN was, until June 1988, trading under the name of Nosey Parkers, an inappropriate title for one of the City's oldest drinking establishments. It was the first public house built outside the city walls. It had always conducted business under the name of the Bishop Blaize Inn, taking its name from the patron saint of the wool-combers. The saint was martyred by the horrible process of having his flesh ripped off by wool-combers' rakes. Today the public house has regained its name and has been refurbished. The lower leat ran right outside the front door and a small bridge, seen in this photograph, was crossed to enter the pub. The leat has been filled in and at present clients sitting outside on the wooden benches will be sitting on what was once a running leat operating some of the city's ancient mills. *c.*1960.

THE AXMINSTER INN, demolished in 1964, marked the end of the old Paris Street. The inn faced 'The Triangle', a piece of land at one time with trees on its perimeter and a fence around it. The area still exists, but is not quite recognisable. The Axminster Inn & the hairdresser took up the whole corner of Paris Street to Russell Street. The latter street has been completely removed, but an indication can be seen where the access road continues to W.H. Smith Wholesalers. Photograph dated 1 January 1954.

In 1955 the Axminster Inn was involved in a flooding disaster. During a heavy rainstorm, water poured along Paris Street, gathering momentum, until the water-level reached around 4 feet. The sewers were unable to cope with the large quantities of water and the inn and the hairdressers were flooded out and all their ground-floor furniture and fittings ruined. A neighbour struggled in water up to his chest and the landlady of the Axminster Inn found her three goldfish swimming near the front door.

ENTRANCE TO WILLEYS, Water Lane, 22 February 1961. As one of the city's largest employers, the company of Willeys was well known throughout Exeter. The company had been formed in 1861. In the early years, the company was connected with the woollen industry, but was to be transformed into a gas and electrical specialists and Willeys were pioneers in a number of aspects relating to the gas industry. In the 1860s the business moved from Shilhay to Water Lane where a 15-acre site was occupied. The company was in many ways ahead of its time and actually produced its own company house magazine called *Willeys Weekly*. Mr Willey wrote in the magazine: 'The ambitions and aims of my life have been to help and benefit the working man.'

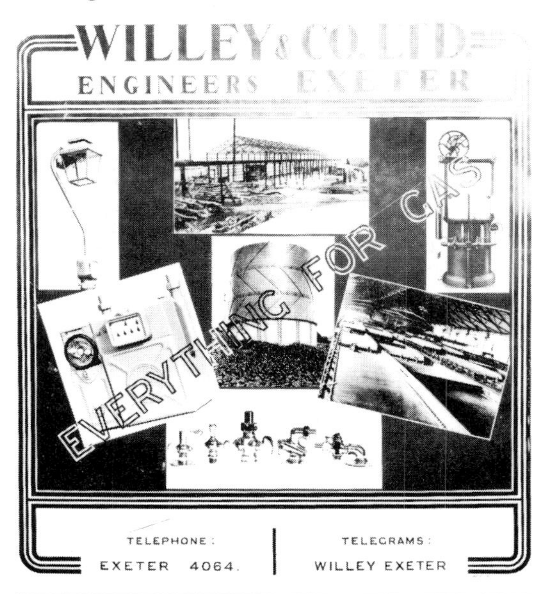

XMAS CELEBRATIONS, Willeys, 20 December 1955.

WILLEYS STAFF, 1941.

CASTING OPERATIONS – Willeys, 18 April 1962. Willeys often specialised in the production of large objects and provided some of the most extensive installations of gas plant in the country. Thousands of houses in England used gas fittings produced at the plant in Exeter. Heavy engineering, iron and steel constructional work, machine hods, stores lighting and the famous gas slot meter originated from Willeys. At one time the company had around 1300 employees including 400 women to assist with the production of war weapons and parts in the Second World War. In 1969 the labour force was 250, but in its heyday the average number of workers was around 600.

CONSTRUCTION WORK, 19 December 1956. Construction of a large metal cylinder at the Willeys works.

REMOVAL OF THE LARGE CYLINDER from Willeys, 4 January 1961.

WILLEYS OLD MACHINE SHOP, 22 February 1961. Much of the machinery used by Willeys became outmoded by the 1980s and a substantial modernisation scheme took place in 1981. The result of the upgrading would double the output of the foundry. The complete refurbishing programme was to cost in the region of £750,000 and was staged in two parts. Much of the heavy manual work was to be eliminated by the use of mechanical handling equipment.

STREET LAMP, Topsham Road, 1 April 1940. The installation of a new street lamp in Topsham Road.

FEMALE MACHINE OPERATOR at Willeys, 18 April 1962.

WATER CLOSET, 2 May 1949. Do you still have one? A large number of these would have been supplied to Exeter houses. Extensive brass foundries produced the base material for the production of hundreds of different fittings for use in the gas industry; cocks, pendants, chandeliers, etc., were available in a variety of differing styles. Henry Wykes undertook a substantial commission to photographically record the many products of the company.

SLOT GAS METER, 25 September 1947. The famous gas slot meter was probably Willeys' best-known product. The company utilised further premises in James Street for the production of their gas meters, and large quantities of station meters, consumer meters and 'penny in the slot' meters were manufactured.

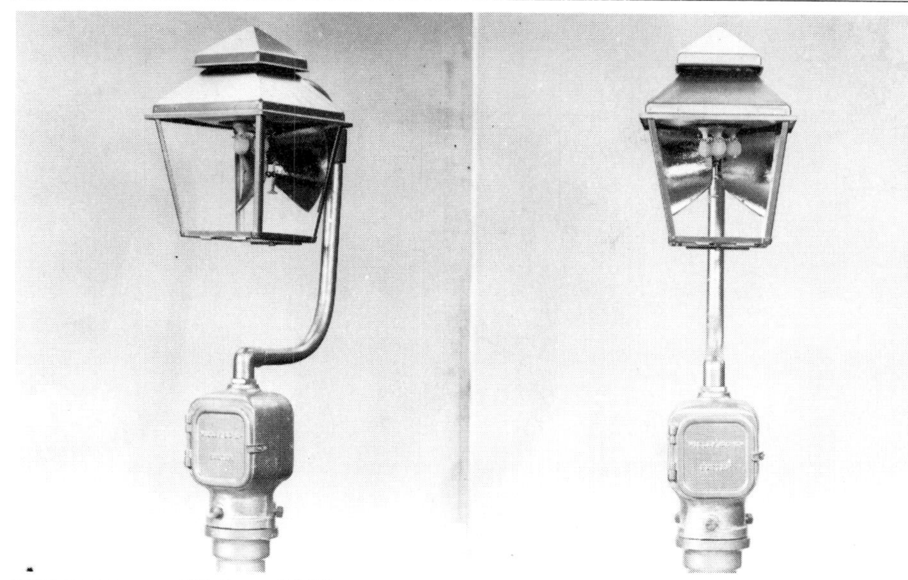

SINGLE GAS LAMP, 25 June 1948.

DOUBLE GAS LAMP, 12 August 1947. The dimly-lit streets of Exeter were to come to life with a Willeys street lamp! This was just one of the many products to originate from Willeys.

BEACH BROS WORKSHOP, 1 March 1949. Manufacturers of corks, bungs and cork products, situated in Western Road, St Thomas, Beach Bros have played a fascinating role in the history of Exeter from 1940. An unusual company specialising in cork products, its history dates back to 1868 when the founder, John Beach, started up in business in Dover. Corks were made for medicine bottles, beer casks and bottled beers. The work was carried out by hand. At a later date, wooden bungs were produced thanks to the aid of new machinery, and the company was to extend its interests into fishing net floats, life belts and sheet virgin cork. It went from strength to strength and its products were in heavy demand during the First World War. With the decline of the cork industry during the twenties and thirties, the company expanded into timber and associated products.

In 1940 the company was ordered out of Dover by the Ministry of Production. It had been making a number of products for the War Office and the Admiralty and 48 hours notice was given to leave Dover, where it had been established for 72 years. During those early years in Exeter the company was to operate from 17 different addresses until the site at Western Road St Thomas was purchased. After leaving Dover it took 2½ years to move all the wood and cork stock to Exeter. All of the staff had to be evacuated to Exeter complete with families, and one can only surmise the problems which this company had been involved in. It is not possible to condense the history of this company on these pages, but an excellent account has been published by its managing director, William P. Beach, entitled *The History of Beach Bros Ltd. 1868–1986.*

BEACH BROS STAFF, 1 March 1949.

HIGH STREET, north side, post-war, 7 July 1953. The rebuilt High Street was to reflect a completely different style from its pre-war character. The pavements were wide, the architecture continuous in style and dominating. The wide variety of smaller shops were gone, being replaced by larger spacious units. The central area of the rebuilt city was to conflict with many buildings around its perimeter and, sadly, over time many of these character buildings were to be removed in the name of improvement.

HIGH STREET, north side. Commercial Union Building, 5 March 1952. The Commercial Union was one of the larger companies which obtained an important city centre site in High Street. The entrance to its offices is seen between the two shops. In the foyer of the Commercial Union offices a space was created for the remnants of the statue of Henry VII that originally stood on the impressive facade of the company's original building in High Street. Only a bust of the king remains, despite the fact that photographic records showed the whole statue still intact after the Second World War. Perhaps the statue was dropped during its move from its lofty perch. The shop on the left is occupied by Kendalls rainwear and umbrellas and on the right Thomas Cook & Son World Travel Service.

HIGH STREET, south side, post-war, but date unknown. The south side of High Street is still to be completed. In the centre of the building is the arcade leading through into Princesshay. On the far right is Timothy Whites the chemist and in its upstairs windows prams are displayed. Further along the street Daniel Neals have moved in, together with a Paige shop, Liptons and Tru Form. At this time the road is not divided through its centre by a narrow flower bed.

CENTRAL HIGH STREET showing the junction of High Street and Castle Street, 13 May 1955. The Westminster Bank has taken the corner site of Castle Street with Lennards shoe shop underneath adjoining McGaheys, the tobacconist. Marks & Spencer, which was opened in 1951, takes the opposite corner. At this time the end of Sidwell Street has not been developed.

HIGH STREET, Nos. 250–1, 13 September 1954. Three Union Jacks fly above Mark Rowe's new store in High Street. To the left is the Scotch Wool and Hosiery Stores. This company had before the blitz been on the corner of the London Inn Square. To the right of the photograph can be seen the end section of Northernhay Place leading to Northernhay Gardens. A substantial section of lower Northernhay Place was blitzed, allowing for the post-war creation of Bailey Street.

UPPER HIGH STREET, 26 October 1964. This record shows Upper High Street looking towards Sidwell Street. Debenhams Store had been completed and opened by the mayor on 5 March 1964. Eastgate House, taking its name from the old city gate, displays the figure of Henry VII. Originally the East Gate supported a statue of the king in an alcove outside. During the period 1962 to 1974 the upper section of High Street was a dual carriageway with a flower-bed running the length of the newly-widened street.

LOOKING ALONG PRINCESSHAY, 10 July 1959. Princesshay was nearly complete. The arcade had been finished in 1957/8 and the paving of the area between High Street and the Post Office was completed in 1960/1. At the top of Princesshay runs a line of crazy-paving which marks where the city wall was demolished after the War. It was removed to allow the completion of Post Office Street.

HIGH STREET, from London Inn Square, looking towards Princesshay on the left, 13 May 1955. The gradual filling in of shops was taking place. Wolfe & Hollander, the furniture shop, has taken the large corner premises with Singers sewing machine shop behind. At this stage Princesshay had yet to be completed and to the left of Singers the city wall is seen with a large gap in it. Originally there was an arch in the wall, but this was removed and the section enlarged to allow access to Southernhay. A small flower-bed has been created also on the left, with Heavitree stone dwarf walls. These small walls enclosing gardens were to become a feature in the rebuilt city centre.

FORE STREET, Nos. 82–3, 16 May 1955. The area of South Street and Fore Street had sustained heavy damage during bombing in 1942. As part of the redevelopment of the city, the section which included South Street, Coombe Street, Sun Street, Guinea Street, George Street, Market Street and Milk Street together with Fore Street, all came under new plans for changes in Exeter. The old Lower Market lay empty and gutted, and children from the surrounding area often played in the large ruin. Eventually the remains of the market were pulled down and replaced by St Georges Market. Nos. 82 and 83 were the first to be built facing Fore Street, the main street. Henry Turner, household furnishers established for many years in the city, and Weaver to Wearer tailors occupied the premises.

Bottom, right.

BRITISH HOME STORES, 11 April 1954. Opened in 1951, British Home Stores occupied a large site at the top of Fore Street on the north side. The site, which had been blitzed, had before the war been a home for the Maypole Dairy, a Gospel Hall and Marks & Spencers. This was originally only intended to be a temporary premises and backed on to the Gaumont Cinema. The building was designed as a ground-floor facility and was adjacent to Brocks the Furnishers. However, the temporary premises were retained and incorporated into a new larger structure. That first construction remains today and is seen on the right side of the present building. In 1980 the design of British Home Stores was seen as unsatisfactory and it was suggested that it should be more in keeping with adjacent properties. However, despite its unsympathetic design, it has remained.

POOLES FURNITURE, RADIO AND TELEVISION SPECIALISTS, were opposite Henry Turners, 2 May 1955. Large lettering over their doorway shows they were established in 1884. They are offering a 'Free Gift' of a tea-set, exchanging old furniture for new, and giving credit. A lady is busy cleaning the door handles. Next door is 'Vanes', specialists in socks and stockings. Olivers shoe shop is adjacent to them. On the left is Mary Arches Street, now greatly widened. Previously it had been an extremely narrow cobbled street.

SANDERSONS, Blackboy Road, 2 July 1962. Built between the old site of the omnibus depot and Grosvenor Place, these large premises were utilised by Sandersons, the wallpaper and paint specialists. Large showrooms, office and a trade department were part of the complex. The actual building was fitted in between Silver Lane and Salem Place.

SANDERSONS STORE, 1962.

MAC FISHERIES, Sidwell Street, 5 September 1954. As part of the rebuilding of Sidwell Street, new shops open up for business. No. 41 Sidwell Street is taken by Mac Fisheries. Eveleighs Garage is seen in the background.

THE JUNCTION OF QUEEN STREET WITH HIGH STREET looking towards London Inn Square, 5 May 1953. This record of the city shows life still continuing amid the remnants of former buildings. On the far right is Barratts shoe shop, a historic double-gabled building of some antiquity that was later demolished.

COLSONS, High Street, on 20 September 1949, after the demolition of Barratts shoe shop. Part of the original frontage still stands, but the main structure of the new building is seen to the left. A large sign on the front of the new section shows the name of the architects: F.W. Beech & E. Curnow Cooks, 15 Dixs Field. All sub-contractors are listed. Following the demolition of Barratts, the general public could look right through the gap to view the cathedral. The contractors were M.T. Sleeman of Longbrook Terrace.

COLSONS, 5 May 1953. 'The transition between the old and new.' The central entrance is that of Colsons with a new shop under the name of 'Modelia' to the left.

CATHERINE STREET, 6 December 1958, the rear of Colsons in Catherine Street. It is unfortunate that this important link between the Cathedral Close and Bedford Street has lost all its character buildings and today there is little to inspire visitors except the ruins of St Catherine's Almshouses. This area lends itself to new development and in 1988 there are plans to revitalise and landscape the ancient back street. These rear elevations were later removed.

COLSONS furniture department, 19 May 1960.

THE CHILDREN'S DEPARTMENT, Colsons, 13 May 1949.

COLSONS RESTAURANT, 6 December 1958.

COLSONS IN-STORE PROMOTION, 'Fabrics into fashion', 29 April 1949.

COLSONS MANNEQUINS, 23 February 1948.

DOES THIS SUIT MADAME? 23 February 1948. Trying on the year's fashion at Colsons.

THE PERFECT FASHION, 29 April 1949.

COLSONS 'FESTIVAL OF FLOWER AND FASHION', 14 July 1950. To assist in this event and to arouse curiosity a London flower-seller is engaged to attract custom.

FASHION MODEL, 23 February 1948.

COLSONS GOWN DEPARTMENT, 16 May 1951.

WINDOW DISPLAY AT COLSONS, 4 September 1952. The promoted colour for autumn is sherry – so an intriguing window display is mounted based on Harvey sherry bottles which are suspended from the showcase ceiling. A notice declares 'Uncorked for Autumn – Sherry – The new colour'. A notice at the rear of the window advertises Colsons Autumn Fashion Parade, in the new restaurant 9, 10 and 11 September, at 10.30 a.m. and 3 p.m. Tickets 2*s* 6*d* from the suit department, first floor. All garments shown in these parades were to be from existing stock.

BARRATTS, High Street.

EXETER HIGH STREET from the junction of Queen Street looking towards the London Inn Square, 1938. With the post-war development of Exeter from the 1950s onwards, Upper High Street was to be recreated in a very different form to that seen here. The original width of High Street was to be doubled and set back from the previous road edge. This photograph shows a variety of architectural styles and businesses. From the left are seen Boots, the *Western Morning News* offices, Ross the tailors, Timothy Whites, J. Lyons and Co., a tobacconists and Wheatons the stationers. From Lyons and Co., all buildings were destroyed or pulled down. On the right side of the photograph is the turning into Martins Lane with the Midland Bank on the corner. The lamppost has a sign with directions for the official Information Bureau at 18 Queen Street on the corner of Paul Street.

Bottom right.
THE SITE OF WHEATONS, High Street, 15 November 1953. The previous record had shown the original Wheatons buildings in High Street, but the business was blitzed. A board placed on the cleared site is the only indication that the shop ever existed. Opposite Wheatons was Bobbys Store and another board states 'Until May 1942 Bobbys of Exeter stood here. Now this famous store and restaurant serves from its temporary premises in Fore Street.' A sign to the right, beside the Colsons sign, also identifies that this site belonged to Cann Bros. The Bobbys and Canns site were to be rebuilt upon, providing a bookshop and a fashion shop. A telephone box was placed beside the tower of St Stephen's Church. The view through the cleared bombed sites looks into Catherine Street.

ROOFTOPS, High Street, 6 July 1951. It is very unusual to obtain records of rooftops and views from roofs. Here Henry Wykes has recorded the scene above Waltons. These kinds of views have mostly disappeared from the central area of Exeter. On the left-hand side can be seen a wooden shed and a labyrinth of iron staircases connects one building with another. In Queen Street one could walk right along the rooftops. Such places were used for fire duty in the Second World War.

THE INTERIOR AND EXTERIOR OF WYMANS BOOKSHOP, 27 February 1952. No. 30 High Street. Built on the pre-war Bobbys site, Wymans Bookshop ran a special lounge on the first floor for their book club members. Items such as maps, guides, view cards, fountain pens, books and general holiday requisites were also sold.

DENNIS DAVIS CARS, 15 November 1953. To reinstate commercial business in the city after the last war, temporary shops were erected to accommodate traders who had lost their own premises in the blitz. Twenty of these units ran across the top of Princesshay. Their life-span was about 10–15 years. A variety of businesses operated from the shops including Dennis Davis cars. This photograph records, from left to right, an Austin Somerset and two MG models. Part of the city wall still stood for some time after the construction of these units, but was eventually removed. Coloured paving slabs were used in front of these shops to make shopping easier.

THE YWCA, Nos. 3 & 4 Dixs Field, is shown in a derelict state on 6 November 1946. Occupying a prime site in the city, these fine buildings were to be seen on the left when entering Dixs Field. This exclusive cul-de-sac was constructed with fine houses on each side with a central garden during the early nineteenth century. The origins of the YWCA can be traced back to 1878 when a reading room was opened for girls to have tea and meet on Sundays. Further records show that 10 Southernhay East was also utilised. In 1906 Nos. 3 & 4 Dixs Field were acquired. It was here that a home and institute were founded together with a Prayer Union Branch and bible classes. In the 1920s a resident paid one pound per week and shared a dormitory with two others. The fee included meals, and morning and evening prayers were compulsory.

WALTONS CORSET WEEK, 20 March 1952. Waltons of Exeter, one of the largest family department stores in Exeter, was perhaps best known for the Fairy Grotto where children could meet Father Christmas. In 1905 George Walton Turner opened a small shop at 215 High Street and from this beginning developed one of the largest businesses in the city. By 1972 Waltons had occupied a substantial section of the city centre, incorporating High Street, Queen Street and Goldsmith Street frontages. Turner died in 1940, but the company continued under the direction of his sons. Waltons was made a private limited company in 1950. The store was substantially refurbished in the 1960s having new front display windows fitted. In 1972, however, Waltons closed its city-centre store, making 180 workers redundant out of their 250 staff. The leasehold was sold to Laing Developments Ltd. and today the site is occupied by Marks & Spencer. The chairman and managing director, Ian Walton Turner, declared that the future for the company lay in supermarkets. The premises of Waltons were at the time in a state of poor repair and several of the frontages were classified as being listed of architectural interest. Some aspects of this architecture was however to be recreated in concrete as part of the new Marks & Spencer building.

WILLIAM BRUFORD & SON LTD., goldsmiths & silversmiths, are today associated with their substantial High Street premises. However, with the loss of their pre-war premises in 1942, Brufords acquired temporary premises at 5 Central Station Buildings, seen here on 8 September 1955. They remained here until 1957 when they moved to their present shop, 1 Bedford Street. Albert Bruford came to Exeter in 1898 and bought out a jewellery business at 241 High Street known as Pipers. This company had been established in 1721. The premises were originally the home of the Earls of Morley and contained 20 magnificent pannelled rooms. They provided a superb setting for Brufords antique silver, gold, furniture and precious jewellery. The premises were totally destroyed in the blitz of 1942. The most predominate feature of 241 High Street was its splendid clock mounted on the shoulders of Old Father Time which overhung the pavement from the first-floor frontage. In 1924 Brufords took over another well-known Exeter company, that of Ellet Lake of 43 High Street. Mr Lake, who retired, had run the business since 1833.

HALIFAX BUILDING SOCIETY, Queen Street, 28 January 1948. The small beginnings of one of the city's largest building societies, in Queen Street. The society now operates from the prestigious building at Broadgate – the 'Old City Bank'.

BROOKINGS, Waterbeer Street, 8 September 1955. For many Exeter people the business of Brooking & Son in Waterbeer Street could have been a life-saver. Conducting its business from Nos. 17–19, the company were jewellers, goldsmiths, watchmakers and supplied electrical goods. More importantly, however, they were pawn brokers. A feature of Gandy Street was the sign of the pawn broker, three large balls suspended from an arm which overhung the pavement. In this photograph the window contains a large amount of silver items, classic teapots on stands, cream jugs, goblets, coffee pots, candlesticks, sugar bowls, cake stands and plates. Three small posters in the window advertise 'Gold Coins'. Some bronze statues are on display and the company's opening times are shown as 9 a.m. to 5 p.m.

THE QUEEN FACADE OF THE HIGHER MARKET. This photograph was taken for the express purpose of recording this building for the Society for the Protection of Ancient Buildings. The Goldsmith Street façade was also photographed. Shops have since been built between the columns of the building. To the left is seen H. Quick & Co., wholesale leather merchants; a poster to the side shows a policeman stating 'You must help reduce road accidents'; rows of secondhand books are inside the entrance to the market; a poster shows *Snow White and the Seven Dwarfs* at the Palladium; a flower-seller stands on the steps with daffodils and Greenslades Tours display a huge painted scene of Dartmoor at their booking office. Outside Madame James is the van of the Devon Tyre Service of Newton Abbott. R.H. Soper, flower-seller, occupies the centre steps adjacent to the West of England Rubber Co.

UPPER QUEEN STREET, 9 April 1955. The time by Farrs the hosiers' clock is 9.50 a.m. (seen far left) and the photograph records Upper Queen Street as seen from the steps of the Higher Market. It shows clearly the junction of Queen Street with High Street, before the demolition of the section of buildings from Little Queen Street to High Street for the construction of the new C & A shop. Trading at this time in Queen Street was Joshua Daw, tailors, Rileys, gents hairdresser, Halifax Building Society, Navanna Photographic Studios, a dry cleaners and the Queens Hotel. Lewis the tobacconist is on the far corner of Little Queen Street.

CANNS, Queen Street, 4 May 1949. The well-known company of Canns started in a small way in Catherine Street in 1896, progressing to Bampfylde Street where a shop was rented for £18 per year. Mr C.W. Cann, joined by his brother Robert, bought 31 High Street in 1900. A highly successful tailoring business flourished and in 1916 Robert Cann retired. Soon afterwards the store started to sell ladies' 'ready to wear'. By 1930 both sons had joined C.W. Cann in his business. Expansion quickly took place and further shops were bought in Taunton. In 1931/2, a men's tailoring business was opened at 4 & 5 Queen Street which the younger son managed. In 1937 the properties of 30 & 31 High Street were joined into one. These buildings were destroyed during the 1942 blitz. All business was then conducted from Queen Street, numbers, 4, 5, 6 & 7. The building of Marks & Spencer, however, marked the end of Canns in Queen Street and the company now operates from Princesshay.

GOLDSMITH STREET, 29 November 1938. At one time it was possible to walk from High Street in a straight line to Paul Street through one of the city's most ancient thoroughfares, Goldsmith Street. Today the street has been practically lost and only one building that originally stood there still exists. As part of the development of the city centre, this was a very regrettable situation as the little street could have been integrated into the scheme instead of being swept away almost completely. Certainly the city has learnt from some of its mistakes, but when whole streets are removed complete with their buildings, any action is far too late.

HIGHER MARKET, Goldsmith Street, 29 November 1938. View of the rear entrance of the Higher Market showing the original steps and iron railings leading up into the building. This was all part of the original design, but these aspects have been completely lost as the ground level was raised considerably losing nearly 6ft. from the bottom of the building. Today this area forms a pedestrian square in the Guildhall shopping centre.

MIDLAND BANK, High Street, at the corner with Martins Lane, 7 August 1948. The junction of High Street and Queen Street shows the old Midland Bank with a large board over the front door advertising 'Buy defence bonds, safe and secure'. The premises, typical of the style found in other buildings in the city, were later to be removed and replaced with a modern structure. The adjoining building to the left, Barratts, was also demolished. On the right-hand side of Martins Lane is Hill, Palmer & Edwards, bakers. On the railings outside the bank a small notice states 'The Salvation Army Forces Army Canteen, Red Shield Club'. The elegant arched lamppost carries a sign for the Information Bureau, Queen Street. On the far left another lamppost still carries the overhead arm for electric trams.

VICTORIA HOUSE, the premises of Messrs Rowe Bros, shown here on 9 May 1950, was built after the disastrous fire which burnt down the Victoria Hall. It had originally stood on the site after the 1914–18 war. Rowe Bros were established around 1850, and specialized in supplying the sanitary and plumbing trade as well as the oil and colour trade. Their premises were in Fore Street and at 192 High Street. They manufactured lead pipe in Waterbeer Street. The new premises in Queen Street proved highly successful, with the company expanding into Bristol, Birmingham, Liverpool and London with subsidiaries in Bridgend and Blackpool. Within the building today are some interesting windows containing stained glass illustrations relating to the other branches connected with the Exeter company.

ROWE BROS & CO. LTD., Queen Street. Rear view, 9 May 1950.

AN INTERIOR SHOWROOM of Rowe Bros on 9 May 1950 displaying cookers and other appliances. In 1942 part of Victoria House was given over to a local bank which lost its premises during the blitz. Taking over a section of a basement the bank continued in business, but eventually moved into Rowe Bros' new extension at the rear of Victoria House where they remained until 1953.

EASTMANS – an exterior view of the premises in Alphington Street, 5 June 1949. This decorated classic shop-front was the ideal showcase for Eastmans' 'white puddings at 1/4 lb, black puddings at 1/- lb', fresh pork pies, sausages, french brawn, cranberry and apple pudding, Montrose pâté and other such delicacies. Registration for bacon and eggs welcomed and emergency coupons.

INTERNATIONAL STORE WINDOW, 6 December 1951. The store in Goldsmith Street displays its wares for the Christmas trade. Cheeses, butter and meats are shown at competitive prices. Hanging up with the holly are four large carcasses with tickets showing 'Choice gammon – the very best – finest selected'. Tinned hams, Prima (product of South Africa), Cheese 1*s.* 2*d.* per pound, pure lard 1*s.* 4*d.* per pound, Golden Downs butter 2*s.* 6*d.*, special Swiss processed cheeses in presentation packs and pasteurised processed American cheese are all shown in the window.

MARK ROWE SHOWROOM, High Street, 16 August 1954. Known as the 'complete house furnishers', the company's early adverts give some surprising facts. The company was the first to introduce American ash, American walnut, and satin walnut into furniture for the west of England. They made their own bedroom furniture and could furnish throughout a palace or cottage, or anything in between the two! A special feature of the company was its wool and hair mattresses and also feather beds. The original premises in High Street were known as Belfast House, because of the Irish origin of the linen used by the company. They also undertook valuations on property and had a depository in Longbrook Street.

MARK ROWE DEPOSITORY, Longbrook Street, 15 May 1950.

THE LARGE EXETER STORE OF BOOTS today stands on what was a line of buildings which stretched from High Street to the entrance of Northernhay Gardens. The position from which this photograph was taken is at the present time a partially constructed office and shop premises, part of which until recently was the ABC Cinema. The photograph is looking towards the side of the Boots building which stands today. The Plaza Cinema looked into the London Inn Square and to the right would have been the New London Hotel. The Plaza Cinema opened on 16 February 1931 with *The King of Jazz* with Paul Whiteman and his orchestra, plus *Sally* starring Marilyn Miller. The Plaza was reputed to have had the first neon sign in Exeter. During its lifetime the building was utilised as subscription rooms and the Hippodrome Theatre. When the building was first erected, a deep tunnel was uncovered while the foundations were being prepared. It was related to a siege of the castle in 1136.

CONSTITUTIONAL CLUB, Bedford Street, 17 January 1939. In 1939 changes are taking place in Bedford Street to accommodate a new branch of Martins Bank Ltd. The ground floor of the building containing the Constitutional Club is being refurbished to the standards required by the bank. The contractors were M.T. Sleeman and the architects Henry Budgeon of Cardiff and Lucas Roberts & Brown of Exeter. Old Catherine Street is seen to the right with Hughes Garage a little further down the street. The main public toilets were situated in Bedford Street with the ladies and gentlemen seen here complete with ornate railings.

BEDFORD STREET, 22 March 1939. Henry Wykes records the completed changes to the Bedford Street building which now houses Martins Bank. The changes have taken away the original feel and proportions. It is unfortunate that Exeter went through a period of changes which significantly altered some of its historic buildings to the detriment of their original designs. High Street is seen to the left with Catherine Street to the right. Eastmans the butchers are on the corner of Catherine Street.

BARTHOLOMEW STREET EAST, 22 December 1948. An interesting post-war photograph of Bartholomew Street East shows the continuation of buildings along the south side of the street. The city wall is running along the right side. During the years 1952 to 1954 changes took place in this area which resulted in the widening of Mary Arches Street and with it the removal of buildings along the street. Mary Arches Street, previously a very narrow cobbled street, bore no comparison to its former self and the resulting developments left an area with little to recommend it.

ALPHINGTON STREET AND COWICK STREET, 13 May 1955. During 1961/2, the corner of Alphington Street and Cowick Street was demolished as part of the Exe Bridge road improvement scheme.

BEDFORD CIRCUS, 20 May 1938. Perhaps the most significant architectural feature in the pre-war city, with the exception of the cathedral, was Bedford Circus, dominating the centre of Exeter. It was one of Exeter's greatest losses and certainly could have been reinstated despite the war damage it received. Walking from High Street into Bedford Street, one crossed the narrow Catherine Street and entered the Georgian Bedford Circus. The eliptical Circus was constructed with 13 buildings on the left and 9 buildings on the right. The first building on the right was a savings bank and in the centre of the western block was the Bedford Chapel. The statue of Lord Courtenay, now in the square at the top of the street adjoining High Street, faced the entrance, standing on a large plinth with decorated iron railings surrounding it. It was to this classic site that Henry Wykes moved from his Exe Bridge studio.

COMMERCIAL ROAD – The City Brewery and the Kingfisher bag factory, 20 May 1957. A view from Gervase Avenue looking across the River Exe to Commercial Road. The tall building on the far left marks the junction of the road with New Bridge Street. The large white building with the tall chimney is the City Brewery and behind it would have been found the shallow lake and weir which were part of the ancient leat system used to power mills in earlier times. The large building on the right, once used for the production of Kingfisher bags, was taken over by Jourdans Box Manufacturers who were the last occupiers of the building before it was demolished in 1960.

CADBURYS, Fore Street, 3 August 1949. The location of this photograph is today Fore Street News, the newsagent's shop on the right-hand side at the entrance to the arcade in Fore Street. It is appropriate as they sell the famous Cadburys chocolates. This site, No. 109 Fore Street, traded before the turn of the century under the name of the Old Star Iron Stores managed by Messrs Newcombe and Co. retail ironmongers and general builders' merchants. They were also lamp and oil dealers. The extensive building contained 20 showrooms with a goods entrance in Smythen Street. Every aspect of the business was catered for. Cadburys of Bournville took over No. 109 and turned it into a 'Food Hints Centre' (two signs hang in the windows). Free cookery demonstrations were available and a large poster gives details of various events.

WIPPELL BROS & ROW, High Street. Probably taken between the turn of the century and 1910, this photograph, which is a copy, shows the premises of Wippell Bros & Row at 243/4 High Street (to the left). On the right is the Devon and Somerset stores.

NO. 226 HIGH STREET, 2 September 1964. Do you buy the *Express & Echo* from vendors in High Street who stand near Gandy Street? In 1964 your paper would have been purchased from a seller who sat in the entrance of the *Express & Echo*. Not shown in this photograph is the decorated sign which used to hang out over the pavement, although the sign support is still in place. At this time Russells, who sold china, cutlery and porcelain, are using the windows for display purposes. The *Express & Echo* poster declares 'attempt to kill Queen in Canada'.

WOOLWORTH AND MOONS, High Street, 29 May 1955. In the 1980s a great change is taking place among Exeter businesses. Many of the established names have disappeared from the city. This photograph of 1955 shows F.W. Woolworth & Co., who in recent times have left the premises, and in No. 192 High Street Moons, who were radio, TV, record and piano dealers. In the years to come there will be few shop fronts like these left in the city.

SIDWELL STREET, date unknown. Photographs of pre-war Sidwell Street do not exist in any large numbers. This one of Upper Sidwell Street, although damaged, gives a good indication of how a series of buildings would continue in the same style in greater quantities than they do now. The shop canopies were also a feature of the time. Only a small number of these shops exist today on the south side of the street towards the junction of Summerland Street.

OTTONS STAND at Countess Wear, 2 August 1950. Until very recent times Walter Ottons occupied substantial premises at Nos. 135–9 Fore Street. The business specialised in iron and steel supplies for builders and was also a general furnishing ironmongers. The company was one of the longest established in Exeter, starting at 110 Fore Street and No. 135. The loss of Walter Ottons' firm amongst others in the city has exemplified the change away from traditional business in recent years.

JOURDANS BOX FACTORY, Sidwell Street, 15 January 1949. Amongst those who came to Exeter to avoid the consequences of losing their businesses in the Second World War was Mr G.A. Jourdan whose speciality was box manufacture and packaging. The company was engaged in work to assist the war effort. Being connected with the county, Mr Jourdan chose Exeter in which to base an auxiliary factory. A building in Blackboy Road was located and duly purchased. The London base was maintained, but in fact it was the Exeter factory which was bombed! Having assembled a considerably skilled workforce by 1946, Jourdans transferred to one of the first factories at Whipton.

SALVATION ARMY TEMPLE, 31 June 1962. The Salvation Army Temple in Friars Walk has a capacity for holding 2,000 people and originated from a Quaker meeting house built in 1833. Purchased in 1882 by William Booth the founder of the Salvation Army, the towers were added in 1889 and the original meeting house extended. The Army's work in the city started after a small group of concerned citizens from The Total Abstinence Society met in premises in Holloway Street to discuss the work of the Salvation Army. From those early days, the Army has gone from strength to strength and continues its good works in the city.

ACHILLE SERRE, dry cleaners, 80 Fore Street, 22 July 1955. The post-war development of Exeter brought with it faster and newer services. Nos. 80–1 Fore Street at the turn of the century contained the business of Mr E.H. Shephard of City and County Supplies. The building then had a four-storey stone front with a handsome dark-painted double frontage and glass windows reaching nearly to the ground. A profusion of articles for day-to-day use were stocked. The shop was 100ft. deep and 15ft. high, stretching from Fore Street to George Street. A noted line in the store was Mr Shephard's 1*s.* 6*d.* tea.

VULCAN WORKS, 14 February 1957. On the 22 April 1960 it was reported that the Vulcan Stove Company in Water Lane was to close down resulting in the loss of some 180 jobs. The company's director stated that the Vulcan had run at a loss for number of years. To offset its losses the company had designed a new cooker called the 'Devon Queen' which, although incorporating many new features, proved uneconomical to manufacture.

VULCAN WORKS ENAMEL SIGNS, 16 February 1957. Many smokers will remember the enamelled signs produced for Capstan and Woodbine cigarettes. The Vulcan Stove Company is seen here putting the finishing touches to these 'works of art'. Today they are collectors' items. With the merger of Willeys and the Vulcan Stove Company, under the umbrella of United Gas Industries Ltd., over 350 people were employed in these affiliated industries.

TINLEYS STAFF, 10 June 1948. There can be few residents in Exeter who would not be familiar with Tinleys Cafés. The most famous of these is still situated at Broadgate leading into Cathedral Yard. In the 1930s meals were served in the thirteenth-century room. Luncheons cost 1*s*. 4*d*. and 1*s*. 8*d*. There was a 'waffle and quick lunch bar'. Morning coffee, teas and ices were available. Started by Mrs Tinley in 1930 when about two dozen savouries would be baked in one day, in 1965 over 200 dozen savouries were being produced every day at the new bakery in Sidwell Street. After the blitz of 1942 Tinleys Café in Cathedral Yard was felt to be unsafe and so the bakery was moved to Blackboy Road. Business continued at the premises while the whole building was reinforced with steel. The business has again been refurbished and is under new ownership.

VIEW OF THE CANAL, 26 March 1952. In October 1952 an article was written in *Country Life* on the history of Exeter canal and illustrated with photographs taken by Henry Wykes. The cottage shown in the centre of the photograph stood at Kings Arms Sluice and has been demolished. The allotments shown on the right have also disappeared because of the major flood-prevention scheme carried out between the 1960s and 70s. The cottages shown on the left side of the canal were also demolished.

REGENT OIL DEPOT, 6 December 1949. Construction of oil storage tanks on the canal banks for the Regent Oil Company.

REGENT OIL DEPOT, 6 December 1949. View along the canal from the Regent Oil Depot works showing allotments to the left. The area beyond the works is seen as almost open country. It has latterly been taken over and almost eliminated by the Marsh Barton Trading Estate.

THE BASIN, in a copy photograph showing four working vessels. Today the basin accommodates more leisure craft and also the exhibits from the Exeter Maritime Museum. The vast majority of buildings in the background have disappeared from the city skyline since the 1950s.

FERODO LTD., 20 January 1954. For many Exonians today the name on this building may not be too familiar, but in latter years its business titles have been Okies, Roots and The Riverside Club, and it was one of the city's nightclubs. It is apparent when entering the building that its design is a result of its use in entertainment activities as it has a large gallery looking down on to the first floor. Known as the Kings Hall, the building was used initially for 'parish purposes'. It then became one of Exeter's first cinemas and the last of the city's pioneer cinemas before changing eventually to a variety theatre. At the start of the Second World War the building changed again and it was used by J. Wippell and Co. to undertake their work for the Ministry of Aircraft.

INTERIOR OF FERODO LTD., Okehampton Street, 20 January 1954. Stack shelving was introduced into the former cinema to accommodate the company's stock of brake and clutch-linings, stair-treads and Ferogrip fan belts. The fan belts can be seen hanging on the side wall of the balcony on the left-hand side.

THE ADVERT SHEET at the Theatre Royal, 5 December 1947. During the intervals at the Theatre Royal a special advert sheet would be dropped. Photographed at 11.25 a.m. according to the theatre clock (right), this sheet gives interesting details of some of the city's businesses. The ropes and black and white tiles are painted on the screen.

Above, left.
THE FAMOUS THEATRE ROYAL SAFETY CURTAIN, 25 February 1951. Photographed at 10.45 a.m., the safety curtain takes on a dual role to advertise the following Exeter businesses: Cullen Bros, removal and storage contractors; R.B. Fulford, typewriter repair depot; Posybowl, South Street; Standfield & White for batteries; Gaytons Garage; Saunders of Fore Street (bulbs, roses, fruit trees); Stalite signs; the Rootes Group; and P. Pike & Co., Austin distributors. As the result of the terrible fire of 1887 in the Theatre Royal, legislation determined that all theatres in the country would have safety curtains.

ENTRANCE TO THE CIVIC HALL, Queen Street, 15 March 1949. The imposing façades of this building were to be seen in Queen Street and Goldsmith Street. In the late nineteenth century, shop-fronts were inserted into the facade in Queen Street which led to the removal of some of the pilasters. Various businesses were to operate from these shops over the years. This photograph shows, to the left, the West of England Rubber Company. In 1919 the Victoria Hall in Queen Street had burnt to the ground leaving the city with no hall in which to carry on its events. At the suggestion of Mayor P.H. Rowsell the Civic Hall was created from an area occupied by butchers' stalls at the end of the Higher Market near Paul Street. The cost was £6,000 with a seating capacity for 1500.

INTERIOR OF THE CIVIC HALL, 15 March 1949. An unknown personality charms the Exeter audience on the grand piano. Many kinds of entertainment were to take place in the Civic Hall, including concerts, bingo, rock-and-roll evenings, wrestling, boxing and sales exhibitions. Large posters advertising events used to be stuck to the pillars outside.

FASHION SHOW at the Civic Hall, 15 March 1949. Despite further expenditure in 1958 the Civic Hall was not paying its way and in 1962 St George's Hall was opened. It was the conflict between the two halls that eventually led to the closure of the Civic Hall. It was said at the opening of St Georges Hall that the hire charges were too high, but despite this situation the older hall continued to lose money. It was officially closed on 30 June 1970 and was later demolished. One of the last businesses to use the Civic Hall was Grays of Exeter who used it to store tents and erected models for prospective customers. Selling was not allowed. The Chamber of Commerce used the cellars for the storage of Exeter's Christmas lights.

CIVIC HALL, INTERIOR, 15 March 1949. It appears that from the outset the Civic Hall was not going to be a major asset as within 10 years it was referred to as the 'Civic Barn'. Mayor Rowsell stated at its opening that it was to be regarded as 'temporary with greater things to come!' The city architect had described the hall as 'Comfortable looking Hall, broad and spacious and decorated with notable taste.' In the 1930s the city was busying itself with new plans for the future which could have included a new hall. However, war broke out and all plans were dropped. In 1949 a call for the letting fees to be reduced was recorded and the building continued to be heavily criticised. One person described the building as the 'Gloomiest building north of the equator.' Refurbishment took place in the 1950s and in 1954 the hall was converted into 'Old Heidelberg' for the Devon Opera Company's production of *Faust*. In 1955 a new floor was fitted.

Sixteen supporting columns ran throughout the hall and there was a large platform at the end where performances took place. Toilet facilities were considered to be inadequate in the latter years of the hall's life. Adjacent to the Civic Hall at one time was Dellars Cafe which lay between the Paul Street entrance and the corner of Goldsmith Street.

ALLHALLOWS CHURCH, Bartholomew Yard, 22 March 1939. Visiting Bartholomew Yard today one would find no sign of the Victorian church that once stood there. The building which eventually fell into disuse was demolished in 1950. Today only some gravestones, tombs and the gateway to the church exist.

THE INTERIOR OF ALLHALLOWS CHURCH, Bartholomew Yard, 22 March 1939. After the demolition of the church, its font was to be seen in a courtyard behind Bartholomew Yard. It was said that the church was of no special architectural interest.

ST CATHERINE'S PRIORY, date unknown. The retention of the ancient St Catherine's Priory, the origins of which can be traced back to the twelfth century, is due to the enthusiasm and dedication of two individuals. Miss A. Legga Weekes, a well-known historian, proceeded single-handed to save the building after it was threatened with destruction. Arthur Everett, an archaeologist, also joined the fight to protect the priory. Eventually Mr Everett undertook considerable excavations at the site and uncovered early coins, bottles, brass tokens, and a portion of a statue dating from the thirteenth century. Due to the tenacity of this famous pair, the building was eventually purchased by the city council and today is the home of the Stoke Hill Community Association. For a number of years the building had been used as a farm. A number of skeletons were also uncovered during excavations.

ENTERING PALACE GATE from South Street today, one would get no indication that at one time one of Exeter's oldest established businesses carried on its trade there. On the left halfway along stands a large plain-fronted building with a main door having windows on each side. Until 1975 this was the property of Kennaway & Co., one of the oldest wine merchants in the country. The site of the building is said to have been once that of a merchant's house and during the occupation by Kennaways a magnificent carving in oak showed the arms of James I with the words 'Mansion 1615' and 'Rebuilt 1819' incorporated into the design. Mansion Cottages stood at the rear of the building. Other pieces of carving were to be seen which were said to come from 'The Mansion'. Kennaway and Co. started trading in 1743, but the company vacated this historic site in 1975.

PALACE GATE, 1954. This record shows the sign of Kennaways on the front of the building, once known as 'The Mansion'. When compared to the photo on the left some changes can be seen in the design of the front of the building.

EXTENSIVE VAULTS are to be found below the building and proved ideal for the storage of wines. The passage leading down into the vaults passed through an archway in an ancient wall. The archway was said to be Roman, and the wall part of the original fortifications of the city. At one time alterations were carried out in the cellars and Roman remains came to light. It was suggested that the archway was the entrance to subterranean passages used in Roman times. The Kennaway Coat of Arms, seen above the archway, was executed in plaster.

THE CELLARS. With the sale of the premises in 1975 various items relating to the business were sold off. A bottle of pre-Phylloxera Chateau D Y Giveau of 1847 was for sale at 'a suggested price of £65'. A vellum-bound sales ledger dating from 1 July 1886 to 31 December 1887 was sold. Entries had been undertaken in copper plate. A feature in one of the rooms where Kennaways conducted their business was a mace-stand. This decorated iron-work stand was used to hold the city's maces, part of the city regalia, which are carried by the Guildhall Mace Sergeants on ceremonial occasions. William Kennaway had been a former Mayor of Exeter.

THE MALTHOUSE, 6 April 1959. Backing on to the city wall in Bartholomew Street East is the Malthouse of which little appears to be known. It stands at the back of the Crown and Sceptre yard. To the left, atop the city wall, are seen Lants Almshouses which were built in 1763. A delightful collection of small houses, with stable doors, they formed a townscape which could not easily be replaced. Later in 1959 all these buildings were demolished. They were not replaced with any other structure and the site today is just a small garden.

WOODLEYS SHOES, 27 April 1949. No. 162 Fore Street is seen here occupied by Woodleys Shoes who were later to have premises at 238 High Street. St Olaves Church abuts the property to the left. Latterly occupied by a decorators merchants, part of the front facia board was either removed or fell off. Underneath was exposed part of a decorated plaster-work facia with swags of leaves and also a bull's head incorporated into the design.

JOSHUA DAW, a well-known business occupied Nos. 10 and 11. The shop, called The Overcoat House, had the date of 1874 painted in the centre of its first-floor wooden window frame, being the date of its establishment. The windows advertise 'habit maker, ladies' tailor, gentleman's tailor, breeches maker.' Next door to the right was Freeths Tofferies Ltd.: 'The best in the West for all chocolates & confectionery. Special agents for Fullers cakes, confectionery and specialities. Cream ices and ice cream bricks in season.'

WYMANS THE BOOKSHOP – display window, 1 April 1953. *Elizabeth our Queen* by Richard Dimbleby takes pride of place in the window of the High Street store. The book at a price of 12*s*. 6*d* is shown as 'not for sale until March 30th'. Other notices state: 'Note the beauty of the binding', 'Ideal for your friends overseas', 'The souvenir book of the year', 'The book everybody is talking about', '8 Full colour portraits 32 pages of pictures'.

WYMANS WINDOW, High Street, 14 October 1953. Further celebrations in coronation year, for the ascent of Everest. A notice tells the public – 'Buy your copy of the Everest expedition, The *Geographical Magazine* on sale within.' Another poster states: 'The *Geographical Magazine* 7 pages in colour 2/6 – Times Everest Colour supplement 3/6.' The major attraction is '*The Ascent of Everest* by Sir John Hunt and Sir Edmund Hillary, 25*s*. In the front of the window is a 'popular airbed', part of the essential equipment used on the Everest expedition.

INTERNATIONAL STORES, interior, 14 October 1947. The grocery department in the International stores displays cans of pilchards at 1*s*. 6*d*., jars of pickled onions, tomatoes 1*s*. 3*d*. lb, compound cooking fat at 1*s*. lb and National butter at 1*s*. 4*d*. lb. A prominent list on the wall gives maximum retail prices.

MARKS & SPENCER, the cheese counter, 19 February 1940. A splendid array of cheeses to tempt customers in Marks & Spencer at prices you can afford: Krustless Welsh Cheddar 1*s*. 1*d*. per pound, English Cheddar 1*s*. 2*d*. per pound, Kraft rindless 1*s*. 2*d*. per pound, Dutch Gouda 9*d*. per pound, rindless Welsh Cheddar 3½*d*., various cheese pieces from 5½*d*., pork pies are 2½*d*.

LIPTONS, High Street, 4 May 1952, the quality grocers with a coat of arms on either side of its name. The window display shows 'Registration: this way to Lipton for quality, value and civility'. Liptons' coffee and tea are advertised prominently on the door.

MARKS & SPENCER SHOE DEPARTMENT, *c*.1935. A startling difference from the way shoes are displayed today is seen in this undated photograph. The shoes seem to fall into two sections, those at 2*s*. 6*d*. and those at 5*s*.

MOONS, High Street, interior. The latest range of Pye radios and televisions as supplied by Moons of 192 High Street in 1955.

EDDIE CALVERT at Moons, 16 April 1955. To boost sales shops would sometimes invite special guests. Here we see the well-known trumpeter signing autographs for swooning fans in Moons shop, High Street.

ST LOYES COLLEGE, sewing shop, 1948. Without any doubt the founder of St Loyes College in Exeter was a most remarkable lady. The objective of the college was to train the seriously disabled to work side-by-side with able-bodied and for them to receive equal payment. The daughter of General Sir Redvers Buller, Dame Georgianna, a tenacious lady, succeeded superbly and by 1953 over 3,000 men and women had been trained at the college and gone into industry. Initially there was one workshop and 20 trainees. From the original building, Millbrook House, the college continued on a road of expansion. After the Second World War it catered for men and women disabled during hostilities. Fairfield House was acquired and two hostels built: Cherry Tree House and Buller House. Later additions were Springbok House, a reading room and library. Northcott House provided the college with excellent facilities for juniors. All manner of trades are taught at the college and it has certainly been one of Exeter's success stories.

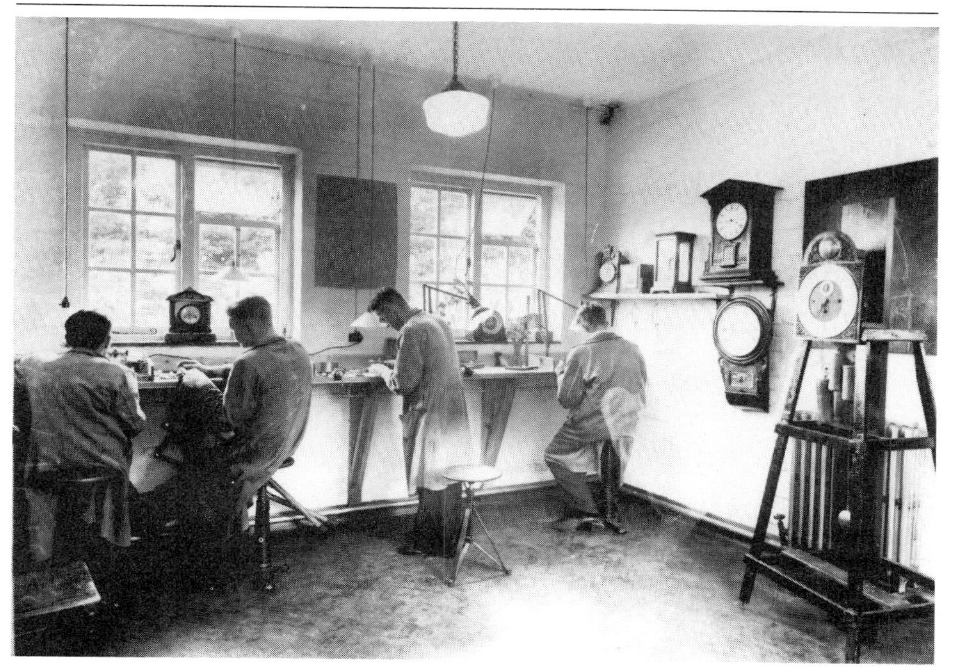

ST LOYES COLLEGE, clock repair department, 1941.

ST LOYES COLLEGE, radio workshop, 1948.

EASTMANS, Queen Street, 14 June 1949. The well-known Exeter butchers, Eastmans, had premises in the Higher Market façade in Queen Street. At this time the company advertise 'North South West, Eastmans are the best, Registrations Welcome.' The window display contains French brawn, fish and meat pastes, New Zealand lamb, amour meat loaf, cucumbers 1*s*. 9*d*. each, luncheon meat and other goods. The shop blind carries the metal badge of Grays of Exeter and the large shop sign is by 'F. Gibbons, Glass Writer 1924.' The window shows the reflection of Little Castle Street on the other side of the road.

NORMANS INTERIOR, 21 April 1938. The interior of J.J. Normans stores, Mount Radford, gives some impression of the range of groceries, wines and spirits which were kept in this prominent establishment. It was the oldest business of its type in the area. Mr Norman acquired the business in 1873 and it was enlarged in 1890. The wine and spirit department, now the Mount Radford pub, was on a site occupied by the old Mount Radford Inn.

MR F.J. BOBBY in 1922 purchased 25/26 High Street and opened a high-class fashion shop. The premises were previously occupied by Greens the drapers and the building contained a magnificent decorated plaster ceiling called the 'Apollo' ceiling. On the retirement of F.J. Bobby, the business was taken over by Debenhams and Bobby and Co. became a subsidiary. Further extensions took place and by 1937 the old printing works of Southwoods in Catherine Street had been purchased and refurbished. A restaurant was added and an orchestra played during dinner and tea. 'Bobbys at this time was Exeter's largest store. In 1942 the premises were destroyed, but trading continued on a much reduced scale in Fore Street. Negotiations took place in 1962 for a new store and building soon started. Some 340 men and 60 sub-contractors were used and a building 140ft. high with seven trading floors was constructed on the Eastgate site. Upon its opening the Sheriff, Mrs Nichols, congratulated the architecture 'on having given Exeter a new line in the skyline' and one she thought enchanting! In 1988 its demolition is being sought.

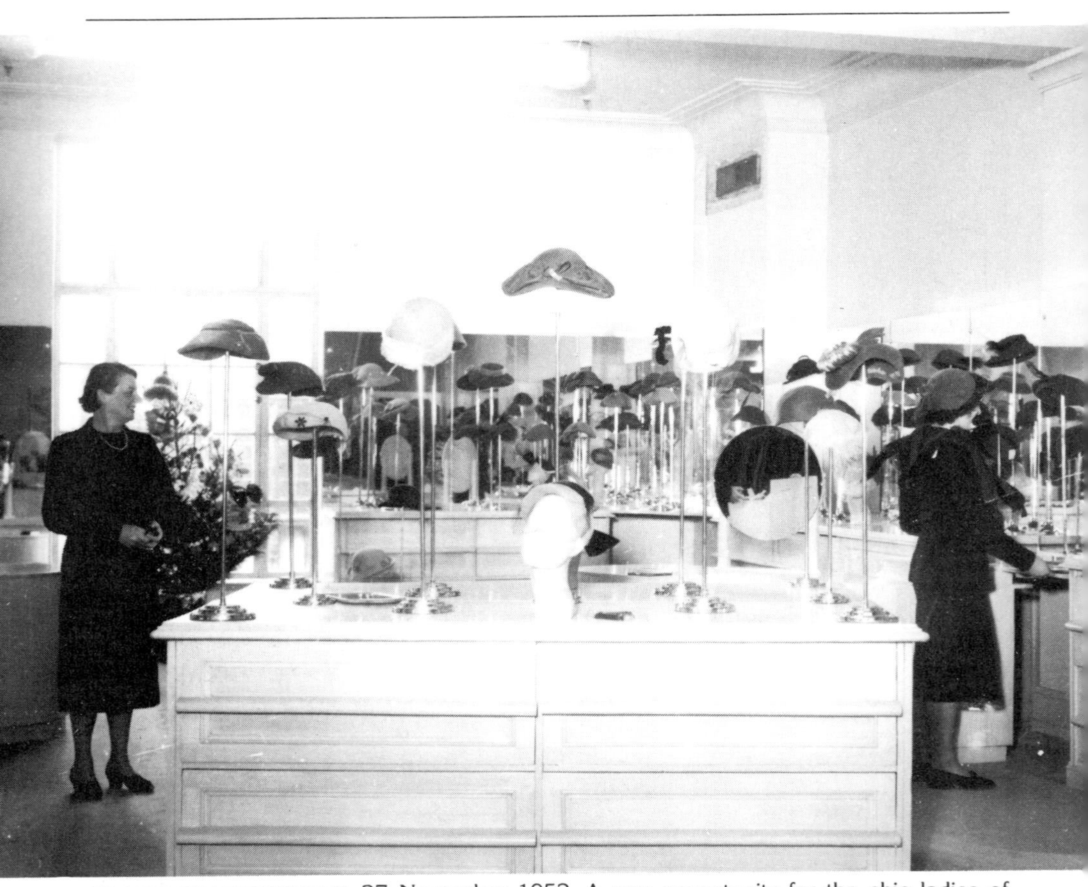

COLSONS HAT DEPARTMENT, 27 November 1952. A new opportunity for the chic ladies of society to buy the latest fashion in hats. The saleswoman assures her client that 'It definitely suits madam.'

Above right.
WALTONS WINDOW – 'Everybody's sewing again'! 26 February 1954. The prominent Exeter store encourages its lady customers to take up the art of needlecraft. This is the age of 'make-it-yourself'. From 24 February to 3 March is the 'Sew and Save Week'. To the left of the window an open book declares 'Your leisure hours at home will be usefully and pleasantly spent creating your own spring outfit. Select your style from our interesting collection of pattern books. All sewing needs are on the ground floor.' Material is shown as 11*s.* 6*d.*, 12*s.* 2*d.*, 13*s.* 11*d.* a yard. Butterick pattern books are on display.

Below right.
WALTONS NATIONAL BABY WEEK, 22 June 1951. A stork flies, baby in beak, over a flowering tree. An addition in the family tree – so the word is 'Dayella for day and night'. Waltons declare 'You will find all the first requirements in our baby shop – First Floor.' Children's dresses are priced from 12*s.* 3*d.* up to 21*s.*

EVERYBODY'S SEWING AGAIN

An Addition
FAMILY TREE!
'Dayella'
for DAY and NIGHT
National Baby Week
'Dayella'

ARMORIAL MANTLEPIECE, Bampfylde House, 14 December 1938. Throughout its history Exeter has provided town residences for county families. Bampfylde House stood on the junction of Bampfylde Street and Catherine Street and was a very solid and substantial building with an enclosed courtyard and porch. The building had few downstairs windows, a measure to offer protection from any unwanted guests. Built in the early seventeenth century the property remained with the Bampfylde family until the death of Georgina Bampfylde in 1914. The house contained oak pannelling and magnificent decorated plaster ceilings. Without doubt the house was one of the city's greatest treasures and in 1933 it was bought by the city council after a most generous offer from its then owner Mr Guest. In the famous Oak Room was one of two chimney pieces found within the building. One had been removed by the first Lord Poltimore, the other which remained was recorded by Henry Wykes. Bampfylde House was blitzed in 1942.

JOHN STREET, 7 January 1947. Looking from Smythen Street to Fore Street. The tower of St John's church is seen still standing on the left. The main body of the church had been demolished in 1937, leaving its tower as the only remnant to show that the building had existed. It stood until 1957 when it was demolished. On the right is No. 109 Fore Street. It appears that at this time a number of premises in Fore Street were empty or certainly in need of restoration.

THE BRITISH RESTAURANT, 109 Fore Street, 7 November 1947. The rear of the premises are shown here in a state of grave disrepair. The condition of the building shown was typical of how the city had left many buildings to deteriorate and such sights have been familiar in very recent times. Certainly Fore Street, which contains a number of buildings with character, has been subject to such neglect. Thankfully today attitudes are different and the city is far more conscious about retaining townscapes and buildings of interest.

WIPPELL BROS. Erected just before the turn of the century, this building facing the Cathedral Close housed one of the city's premier businesses, Messrs J. Wippell and Co. The previous properties on the site had been destroyed by fire. Wippels premises extended from 55 & 56 High Street through to the Close. As manufacturers of church furniture, clerical gowns, communion plate and textile fabrics for church use the premises were ideally suited. The company also traded from 4 & 5 Duncannon Street, Strand, London. In recent years this well-known company has moved from their central position to St Thomas.

HENRY WYNNE TIGHE opened the first shop at 4 High Street in 1850, followed by no. 3 High Street in the 1920s. Both properties were blitzed in 1942. Part of the open-fronted shop of Mock & Son in Martins Lane was then leased. This property was the first in Exeter to have a new shop front after the blitz of 1942. Further generations of the Tighe family continued to run the chemist business.

WALTONS ROOFTOPS, date unknown. An interesting view from the rooftop of Waltons Complex. The reason for the grouping of the building to form a small courtyard is not known. Most of the buildings were about four storeys high. On the right-hand side is an unusual architectural feature resembling a dovecote. It is not known what building this feature was on.

GREENSLADES TOURS, Queen Street, 1925. In 1912 two brothers started a charabanc business which was to become one of the best-known companies for coach touring in this country and abroad. As the company of Greenslades expanded in the 1930s and '40s booking offices were required. In Exeter they obtained premises at 10 Queen Street. On the left are three men, of which two could be the Greenslade Bros. Adverts declare 'Coach Tours on pneumatic tyres', Wednesday 9.15 Dunkerry Beacon, Minehead and Clovelly. Trips to Haytor Rocks and Becky Falls 5/6.'

DEVON AND EXETER INSTITUTION, 3 March 1939. At one time the town house of the Courtenay family, earls of Devon, the Devon and Exeter Institution, as it is known today, is one of the city's architectural and historical gems. The building was in the possession of the Courtenays when it was acquired by the Devon and Exeter Institution for the promotion of science, literature and art. The building dates from c.1450 and was designed around two large courtyards with a large garden and stables at the rear. At the end of the sixteenth century alterations were made. In the early years of the Institution's possession, 'Courtenay House' was altered to accommodate a double library by covering the rear courtyard and garden. The libraries are lit by daylight from the domed glass roofs.

DEVON AND EXETER INSTITUTION, 3 March 1939. The interior of the Institution today houses some 40,000 plus books and other items of great historical significance to the city and county.

BODLEYS FOUNDRY, 16 August 1955. Situated in Shilhay the foundry of Bodley Bros and Co. was established in 1790. It was the oldest foundry firm in the city and today, if it had still existed, would have been worthy of a museum in its own right. The old Quay Foundry was first lit by gas, being adapted for this use around 1800. The company covered many aspects of engineering, brass and iron foundry work. Their speciality was the manufacture of machine-moulded gear-wheels which were supplied all over the world. This wonderful record taken at the foundry shows the size of some of the items made. The company had a very high reputation in their field. One of their famous products was the Bodley Stove which had been invented and patented by the company. It was said 'to meet every demand for an article upon which can be placed every reliance'. When the company closed, machinery was obtained by the Science Museum and a museum in Yorkshire.

HEADWEIR MILL, 26 October 1966. For the visitor to Exeter today perhaps one of the most pleasant places to spend an evening is at the large public house called The Mill on the Exe. Situated at Head Weir, an excellent view of the weir and River Exe is obtained. However, the visitor may not realise how recently it was a working mill. In 1896 fulling mills were advertised to let and they were probably situated at the site shown above. A Mr Edward Pym advertised the fact 'that newly erected mills would manufacture every description of paper'. Mr Pym further stated that 'he would produce the most superior paper in the county'. If part of this mill had not been retained for pleasure purposes there would have been no indication that such commercial activities ever took place. The site also has great significance to Exeter in connection with the city's water supply and the operating of mills from the leat which ran into the lower areas of the city.

EXETER BOWLING CLUB, Barnfield Green, 25 May 1954. The City of Exeter Bowling Club was formed in 1906 when a few enthusiasts decided that a club would give a better opportunity to undertake friendly games with other clubs and among members. A syndicate was formed in 1920 whose members created a company and bought land by taking up debentures. The area purchased was between Denmark Road and Athelstan Road. In 1933 the freehold and property on the land was purchased and the company called the Barnfield Green Co. Ltd. In 1934 a ladies section was formed with many distinctions being gained on the green. The ladies have also been responsible for the provision of refreshments and for the raising of monies through social activities and events. The club continues to prosper today.

WESTERN RADIO, 18 November 1953. In 1942 Mr W.J.A. Spicer left the Royal Air Force after war service and started a small radio workshop at Stepcote Hill. New premises were found at Wonford for renting radio receivers. From 1952 a shop operated in Paris Street. In 1954 Mr and Mrs Spicer were joined by Mr Peter Williams and a company formed. Premises were taken in Eastgate in the form of a temporary prefabricated shop. In 1956 the company offered the first specialist record centre. In 1958 the firm moved to 9 Queen Street. In 1962 Fildews, another radio and TV business, was bought at 99 Fore Street. Westerns also bought 7 Queen Street, but finally came to rest at 180 Sidwell Street.

THE QUEEN MOTHER at Hope Hall, date unknown.

COWICK STREET SCHOOL, 4 June 1949. Getting ready for life? A charming study of two children at Cowick Street School enacting what they might be doing in later life – but what is the significance of the blackened faces?

COWICK STREET SCHOOL, 4 June 1949. A strange mixture for a wedding! A bear with keeper, sailors, a wasp, a cotton picker and a young lady holding a big picture of the sun. But why black faces?

ST THOMAS SCHOOL, 7 July 1947. A wonderful time in Henry Wykes studio! A transformation takes place to create a day at the seaside. Seagulls in the air, sandcastles, buckets and spades, and even a young man playing a banjo.

PUPILS FROM MOUNT ST MARY CONVENT SCHOOL, Palace Gate, rehearse their roles for a play in the school's garden, 27 March 1953. Behind the group can be seen the city wall showing the evergreen oaks which still stand today opposite Dean Clarke House. The origins of this school date back to 1896 when Presentation Nuns arrived at Palace Gate. A school was founded for girls between 11 and 18 based on Roman Catholic educational principles. In 1949 the school was transferred to a site in Wonford Road. Properties adjacent to the school were purchased in the 1950s and a lower school built in the 1960s, together with a main block. In the 1970s a gym hall was constructed. Some of these early buildings are being demolished this year in preparation for the commencement of new building work.

BARTON PLACE NURSERY, 20 May 1941. Situated two miles from Exeter, Barton Place consisted of 140 acres of land on the Cowley Road just north of Exeter. It was selected by a Mr Merrivale in the 1790s, on which to build a fine mansion. It was completed in 1797. At that time the estate only consisted of a small farmhouse which was pulled down. The owner meticulously laid out the gardens of the house, planted woods and designed groves around the building. Barton Place was often referred to as 'Cowley Barton' and no records were made of its building. Its construction was, however, put into the care of a builder named 'Coffin' who eventually married into the family. It was this property that Lord William Gascoyne Cecil, bishop of the diocese, retired to in 1932.

BARTON PLACE SCHOOL, 20 May 1941. In 1942 Barton Place was utilised by the Save the Children Fund and this photograph captures some happy days for youngsters on the lawns of this lovely house during the early days of the Fund's work. The principal of the University College was to take up residence in the mansion and in 1948 the property was acquired by Exeter University.

ST MARGARET'S SCHOOL, 12 May 1955. A booklet called *Memories 1902–1979* gives some interesting and enlightening details about the school 'for the daughters of gentlemen'. Started as a private venture by a mistress of Maynards School in Southernhay at the turn of the century, the school attracted some 50 day girls and 12 boarders by 1903. Often young ladies would be seen sitting under the beech trees in the gardens of Southernhay with their teachers. Concerts and poetry recitals were given at Barnfield Hall. In 1917 the headmistress sold the Southernhay property and transferred the school to Wynlaton, Magdalen Road.

CLASSROOM OF ST MARGARET'S SCHOOL, 12 May 1955. In 1921, due to failing health, the headmistress, Miss Jago, sold the school to a friend, Miss Edmonds. Major improvements took place and in 1928 a new gymnasium was built which also served as a hall. An adjacent house, Baring Lodge, was also purchased, as was Baring House later and by the 1920s the school was well established.

ST MARGARET'S SCHOOL, 12 May 1955. Bedroom for boarders. During the blitz of 1942 the brave action of the staff, acting as air raid wardens and extinguishing incendiary bombs as they fell, saved the school from burning down. During this period accommodation for the girls was found at Bradninch. Later, in the 1950s, girls were discouraged from looking at young men from Exeter School and fraternisation was totally against regulations. Wallpaper was used to block the windows facing Magdalen Road so that young ladies would not be tempted to watch the boys as they walked along this street and Manston Terrace.

COUNTESS WEAR SCHOOL, 28 June 1949. Six enchanting fairies capture the photographer's imagination. Who could fail to be enamoured of these delightful young ladies giving their all for the cameraman?

COUNTESS WEAR SCHOOL, 8 July 1947. Fairies at the bottom of the garden – no fairies in the fields near Countess Wear! This is what dreams are made of!

BRADLEY ROWE SCHOOL, 25 April 1951. Getting ready for Christmas. Bradley Rowe schoolchildren visit 4 Northernhay Place to be recorded for the Christmas play. Eight lovely angels at the rear, the wise men bearing gifts, Mary and Joseph, and of course the crib. One little girl in the front holds the baby while the other, very coy, young lady holds a lamb.

BRADLEY ROWE SCHOOL, 25 April 1951. All boys together – the Bradley Rowe boys football team 1950/51.

WHIPTON SCHOOL, 16 July 1947. Maypole practice for Whipton schoolchildren. Eight boys and eight girls weave their elaborate patterns on the decorated pole.

NEWTOWN SCHOOL, 3 April 1957. A delightful group of local children portray the season of the harvest. From the back left: two seedsmen, three millers, the windmill, three sheaves of corn. Front left: the baker's oven, the cake and two bakers holding loaves of bread.

THE BOYS OF BRAMDEAN SCHOOL visit the restaurant at Colsons, High Street for a slap-up tea, 24 February 1955. Bramdean School, a preparatory school for boys, was founded in 1907 by Mr A.C. Walters BA. A fine schoolmaster with high standards, Mr Walters taught stringent principles of loyalty to God, to one's family, to one's school and fellow students. 'It is the soundest basis on which to guide and build up ideals', Mr Walters was quoted as saying. Tributes to Mr Walters who ran the school with his wife until retirement in 1935, refer to him as 'a great gentleman – honourable, modest and kind and a fine teacher'.

ST SIDWELL'S SCHOOL, 1950. The studio portrays 'The Sleeping Beauty'. The princess, centre, with the prince on a hobby horse, the wicked fairy at the back, four page boys and two young ladies.

EPISCOPAL SCHOOL, 20 June 1949. Situated on the splendid site of Mount Dinham, Episcopal Secondary Modern School had its origins as a charity school started at the beginning of the eighteenth century. The original school was opened in 1709 by the Bishop of Exeter, Dr Offspring Blackall. Here we see pupils from the school undertaking Tyrolean dancing on the lawns at Mount Dinham. For a number of years the headmaster of Episcopal boys school was Mr Badcoe. He was a keen photographer, using the famous Leica camera for his photographic work, and regularly visited Switzerland for which he had a particular fascination. He arranged school trips to the country and also undertook work for Greenslades Tours, who obviously used his photographs to promote their tours there.

LADYSMITH SCHOOL, 16 June 1949. Great artistry has gone into this production of 'Noah's Ark'. The hand-painted cloth ark gives a home to (from the left) an elephant, chimp, giraffe, orang-utan, cat, sheep, hippo, rabbit, kangaroo, cow and lion. The 12 children behind support each painted animal.

CENTRAL SCHOOL, 4 July 1947. Servicing the city centre, Central School was founded in 1811 when premises were secured in Sun Lane for educating children of the poor and for the training of schoolmasters for other parts of the county. The school catered for many of the children brought up in the West Quarter and surrounding area. Situated off Rack Close, access could be gained to the school via a flight of steps from Coombe Street in the latter years. The school was demolished in 1979. The children shown here are photographed in a variety of costumes for a pantomime or Christmas play. Father Christmas is seen far right.

HOLLOWAY STREET SCHOOL. Henry Wykes took this group into Bull Meadow park at the back of Holloway Street School. This group of six girls and four boys are about to set out to sell their wares. The little boy in the back row left carries a tray of sausages, the young lady a tray of bananas, the girl in the centre apples and the boy on the end a dead rabbit! The school was opened in 1876.

ST SIDWELL'S SCHOOL, 9 July 1947. Many people may wonder why there is a triangular garden within Queens Cresent, Longbrook Street and York Road. The reason for it is that it is a secret place and visited by fairies! Here is the only time it has ever been recorded (thanks to St Sidwell's School).

MOUNT RADFORD SCHOOL, established 1872, was a boarding and day school for boys. Teaching was 'assisted by efficient staff and masters'. Separate classes were available 'for small boys under a fully certified Froebel Mistress', according to early school adverts. A yearly booklet *The Radfordian* related to the Old Radfordian Association, and also the school's activities. The 1947 cricket team (above) would have featured in the booklet. In 1904 Theodore Ernest Vine joined the school and later became headmaster from 1916–1957.

HEAVITREE INFANTS SCHOOL, 4 July 1947. The Lion Tamers! Four ferocious lions are kept well under control by their handlers. The costumes for the lions were all hand-knitted in a very coarse wool. Heavitree Church is seen in the background.

MONTGOMERY SCHOOL, 8 July 1947. Set against a hand-painted cloth background depicting a garden, it appears that this playlet is about the spider and the fly. In front of the little tiled cottage sits a young lady with glasses. Dressed in dark clothing she has four long legs, which supplement her own two arms. Judging from her face she is enjoying every minute, but the young man beside her is not amused! Standing with folded arms he is clad in a helmet with two antennae and is obviously going to be her victim. The rest of the group think this is all great fun and a number of them grin, showing their missing teeth.

ST MARY ARCHES SCHOOL, 17 June 1949. A group of 20 majorettes stand on top of the catacombes at the lower cemetery to be recorded for posterity. In front of the two central drummers is a little boy dressed as a clown. Mary Arches School originally stood where the multistorey car park now is in Bartholomew Street East.